EYE JUGGLING

Seeing the World Through a Looking Glass and a Glass Pane

A workbook for clarifying and interpreting values

Rodney Frey

Professor of Anthropology
Lewis-Clark State College

UNIVERSITY
PRESS OF
AMERICA

Lanham • New York • London

Copyright © 1994 by
University Press of America®, Inc.
4720 Boston Way
Lanham, Maryland 20706

3 Henrietta Street
London WC2E 8LU England

Library of Congress Cataloging-in-Publication Data
Frey, Rodney.
Eye juggling : seeing the world through a looking glass and
a glass pane : a workbook for clarifying and interpreting values /
Rodney Frey.
p.   cm.
Includes bibliographical references and index.
1. Values clarification.   I. Title.
BJ66.F74   1994   121'.8—dc20   94–22107 CIP

ISBN 0–8191–9637–1 (pbk. : alk. paper)

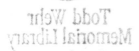

Dedicated to the students:
may they come to better know their own stories
and appreciate those of others.

Contents

Preface

How has humanity, in all its diversity, defined its relationships to animal and plant, to sky and earth, to nature and the world? What are our values and what are the values of others toward nature and the world? How do we come to know and articulate our own values? How do we come to know and appreciate the values of other people? Why do we value our particular view of the world? Why do others value their particular view of the world? And simply put, why do we value what we value? These are among the particular, if ambitious, questions addressed in a course I taught entitled, *Wilderness: An Integrative Seminar*.

After several attempts at more traditional instructional formats, which included extensive reading and writing assignments supplemented by intricate instructor lectures and class discussion or what can be termed, "the-overwhelm-the-student-and-maybe-something-will-sink-in" approach, I decided to re-focus my instructional endeavors. I felt there must be a better way to address the critical questions posed in the seminar. So I dropped the assigned textbooks and wrote up my lecture notes, which were full of illustrative stories and anecdotes.

The resulting endeavor presents an assemblage of "story texts," along with a method of interpretation, as a workbook for values clarification. I hope that by presenting a limited, though densely rich assortment of story texts, that the student and instructor can more effectively explore together and come to appreciate why, as a humanity and as individuals, we value what we value and see the world as we see it.

In the process of writing this workbook, I also decided to attempt a transfer of authority. By offering a methodology of interpretation, I, the instructor, sought to relinquish authority as somehow a source for imparting knowledge and to vest the student with an opportunity to assume much of that authority. With a methodology of interpretation, the student can explore, discover and interpret for him or herself. The student can become an authority of the values and knowledge he or she helps reveal. This workbook should be approached not so much as a source of values and knowledge, but as a strategy for discovering values and knowledge. The question posed is as much *what* is to be learned as *how* is it to be discovered.

A bibliography is offered of the materials that have helped orient and inform my original lectures and stories, and upon which much of this workbook is based.

* * * * *

I wish to give thanks to all the students who have participated in telling and hearing of these stories, to my colleague Patricia Keith, and to Tom Yellowtail and all the Crow and Coeur d'Alene Indian elders who first taught me the art of *eye juggling*. Their concerns, guidance and inspirations gave birth to the writing of this workbook. Their participation and interactions with the stories gave life to its methodology and story texts.

I am also grateful to the following publishers for permission to reprint copyrighted materials: HarperCollins Publishers for materials appearing in *Steps to an Ecology of Mind* by Gregory Bateson, the Delegates of the Oxford University Press and The Syndics of the Cambridge University Press for materials appearing in *The New English Bible* edited by Samuel Sandmel, and the University of Nebraska Press for materials appearing in *Land of the Spotted Eagle* by Luther Standing Eagle.

Rodney Frey

Eye Juggler: An Introduction

There is an old man, with long, black braids. He stands there, beside that tall cedar tree, singing a song. As he sings that song, what should happen..., his eyes pop out of his head. He continues singing that song and his eyes go up the side of the tree to the top branch. There those eyes look to the east. Then they turn and look to the south. The old man with empty sockets in his head continues that song. From the top of the tree the eyes look to the west. And then the eyes turn once more and look to the north, the fourth direction.

As the old man with long, black braids sings that song, who should come along the path there but Coyote, down on his luck.[1] He sees the old man standing there and decides to pay him a visit. He's been out there in those hills a long time. But as Coyote gets a little closer he realizes that there is something odd about this old man. He's seen some strange things out there in those hills but nothing like this. The old man is singing his eyes to the sky!

Now Coyote, who's been down on his luck, realizes a good thing when he sees it. If he had this trick, he could go to town, stand on a street corner and sing his eyes out. He could juggle

---

[1] As with all Coyote stories, this Northern Cheyenne trickster story should only be told aloud during the winter season, from the first frost of fall until the first thunder of spring. This story text is similar to that told in my class and originally based upon a text as found in Thompson 1929:63.

his eyes, and become...an "eye juggler!"   He would certainly become rich then.   That's what Coyote is thinking.

By now the old man with the long, black braids has completed his song, and his eyes have come down the side of the tree back into his head.

"Old man, teach me this trick," Coyote says.

"This is no trick, but a way of seeing the world.   When I send my eyes to the sky, I look in the four directions and only the four.   In that way I show respect to that which I see.   Never try to see too much," the old man says.

"That's fine, but teach me the song anyway," Coyote says.

Well, the old man with the long, black braids has a difficult time saying no to anyone, so he agrees to teach Coyote how to sing his eyes to the sky.   And it turns out that Coyote is a pretty good student and he picks up that song.

But once more the old man with the long, black braids says, "when you sing your eyes to the sky, look in only the four directions.   Never try to see too much."

"Sure, sure," Coyote says, and he's off.   With that song, Coyote is eager to try out his new trick.   He goes that way, into the forest and searches for a tall tree.   No short tree will do.   He searches here and there, trying out all the trees around.   None will do.   Over that hill, there he goes, now along that ridge, further into the forest Coyote wanders, looking for the tallest tree.

After a long and exhausting search, the perfect tree is found. It towers high, touching the clouds.   Coyote begins singing that song, the one I told you about.   And what should happen..., his eyes pop out of his head and go up the side of that tree.   It works!   From the top of the tree the eyes look to the east, to the south, to the west, and finally, to the north.   "I'm going to be famous and rich.   I'm going to be...an eye juggler!" Coyote says.

At the end of the song, the eyes come down the side of the tree and back into Coyote's head.

It's late, and you don't want to get caught in that forest at night.   It's dangerous.   So Coyote begins walking back to his camp.   He goes that way.   Then this way.   But everything is so strange to him. Did he come this way or that? He goes to the top of a high ridge and looks everywhere. Nothing is familiar. He's lost! What's he to do?

Then Coyote remembers his special song. "I'll send my eyes to the sky again, and they'll see a way back home." Coyote sings that song. Just as before his eyes pop out of his head, and go to the top of the tree. One eye looks this way, the other that ways. In all the directions those eyes look..., and then some. And they see the way back to the camp. He'll be safe now.

So the song is sung to its conclusion. It's sung..., and nothing happens! The eyes remain fixed at the top of the tree.

He must've left out a word from the song. So very carefully, Coyote sings that song again. But when the song ends, the eyes are still in the top of that tree.

It's a hot afternoon, and the sun is beating down on those exposed eye balls, and they begin to swell up.

Coyote tries climbing the tree. But he can't see so well, and about half way up he misses a branch and falls to the ground.

Flies in great numbers are landing on those exposed eye balls.

He searches around on the ground and picks up a stone there and that stick here, and throws them to the top of the tree. But when they fall, the eyes remain there, and the stone and stick land on the head of...Coyote!

The crows have found those eyes and are about to have a little afternoon snack.

Coyote lays there, at the base of the tree, crying huge tears from his empty eye sockets.

Just then, Mouse runs across Coyote's face. Maybe he's after a whisker hair for his nest. But as Mouse runs across the face of Coyote, the tail of Mouse falls into the open mouth of Coyote and Coyote immediately closes his mouth tight on the tail of Mouse. Coyote pulls from his mouth that which he's captured. That Coyote is quick!

Now how many working eyes does Mouse have? And how many does he have? "Mouse, younger brother, give me one of your eyes, or that'll be it!" Coyote says.

Now Mouse thinks this over. He's a family man, with several wives and lots of kids. He has responsibilities. His life is very valuable. So very carefully, Mouse pulls out one of his eye balls and hands it to Coyote. True to his word, Coyote lets Mouse go.

Now that eye ball is pretty small. But Coyote puts it into one of his empty sockets. It fits alright. And what should happen..., he can see!

One slight problem. Every time Coyote moves his head, ever so slightly, that eye ball rolls around and around inside that head, and everything looks wobbly and blurred.

But the first thing Coyote sees is Buffalo standing over there. How many working eyes does Buffalo have and what size are they, and what does he have? So Coyote takes out his rifle and goes over to Buffalo. "Buffalo, younger brother, hand over one of your eyes, or that'll be it!" Coyote says.

Now Buffalo thinks this over. And just like Mouse, he's got several wives, lots of kids. He's a family man, with responsibilities. So very carefully he pulls from his head one of his eyes, and hands it to Coyote. True to his word, Coyote lets Buffalo go.

Coyote tries to put the eye in, but it's pretty good size. He turns and twists, but is just won't stick. It falls to the ground, and gets all dirty. Coyote brushes it off and tries again, and again. It just won't stick. So he goes over to a tree and begins pounding his head against the eye ball against the tree..., and eventually it sticks! But that eye ball just hangs there..., half out. And the other one, well, it just rolls around and around and around in that head.

There goes Coyote. You'll certainly recognize him if you come across him in that forest there.

                    * * * * *

This Cheyenne story is often told to help explain why some people just don't see...eye to eye! The story's theme is, of course, about differing ways of seeing the world. With the Eye

Juggler setting the tone of this workbook, I invite you to an adventure in eye juggling.

My premise is rather straightforward. As a humanity, *we are the stories we tell.*[2] In the stories we share with one another, we define the primary qualities of how we came to be, our origins, and what we can become, our destiny. In the stories, we define who we are, what the world is and how we are to relate to that world. Our ways of knowing and our ways of motivating are found in our stories. Through the stories, we learn and re-affirm our basic cultural values of time and space, causation and being, and give meaning to all aspects of our lives. In the stories, *we are.*

We carry forth our stories and with them create our social institutions, our ways of behaving toward each other. Family, church, school, recreation, art, government, economy, science, technology, work are all animated, structured and given meaning through our stories. We celebrate our stories at every opportunity: in Sunday worship at church or at a football stadium, in a graduation commencement or each Friday after work at the local bar, in a class or family reunion, in a hard-earned job promotion or vacation cruise to the Caribbean. We tell our stories at each juncture in our lives: at birth, at each birthday, at marriage, at divorce, at our death. Our lives are inundated with our stories.

We carry forth our stories and with them create our view of the world about us and our ways of behaving toward it. How we define a landscape, the rush of water in a river, a sunset, a thunderstorm, the howl of a coyote, the flight of an eagle, the ant

---

[2]"Story" refers to the fundamental symbols and values, and the distinguishing cultural character pervading a portion or the entirety of a society and its various institutions; what I have come to term, "cultural story." It can be inclusive of both "mythic" as well as "historic" significance. And embedded within our cultural story is the single most important influence on the behaviors we exhibit and the worlds we create, our "values."

that walks across the kitchen table: all are predicated on the stories we tell. Our aesthetic, our religious, our economic and our scientific images of plant, animal, earth, star, and of their origin, dynamics and destiny are framed in our stories. The lives of others are inundated with our stories.

Simply put, our humanity and our world are defined in the stories we tell each other. Without stories there can be no human being, and there is no world.

It follows then that to understand how humanity sees itself and the world, we must learn something about the stories humanity tells. Through an appreciation of the stories, we have access to what is most essential to humanity. To understand "wilderness," for instance, is to go into someone's story of wilderness, and not into a wilderness area. "Wilderness" does not have existence "out there," in nature, but in the symbols and values embedded in someone's story of it.

This workbook will descriptively present an assemblage of distinctive stories. The stories range from an Inuit (Eskimo) creation story to the stories of Pythagoras, Newton, Descartes and Maslow to the stories of quantum physics and cybernetic epistemology; from the story of the walls of Jericho to a story painted on the walls of an Upper Paleolithic cave to the story of Plato's cave. Many of our stories will be framed as "mythic" narratives, e.g., the Australian Aborigine story of Karora, a mythic being. While others are presented as "biographical" or "historical" accounts, e.g., Galileo's life and accomplishments or the theory of human evolution.[3] Some of our stories are to be

---

[3]The term "myth" refers to that which is considered as a "true story" and which offers exemplary meaning and value to life. Myth is not to be considered as "fable," "fiction," or "illusion." The "truth" of a myth is to be appreciated and is expressed metaphorically and anagogically as opposed to empirically. Hence myth is not bound by a history, as part of chronological time, but is considered "timeless," *in illo tempore*, and is imbued with aesthetic and often sacred significance.

The term "history" refers to those factual-based events that have

seen in an artistic sketch, e.g., a drawing by an Inuit shaman, or in an architectural structure, e.g., the Greek Parthenon or a Crow Sun Dance Lodge. And still other stories are expressed in the words of a "poem" or "song," or even in the diagram of a mathematical theorem. Our stories come in many forms, pervading all aspects of our lives.

While some of the stories may seem culturally distant and temporally ancient, I would suggest that they are in fact stories reflective of the *foundations* upon which our contemporary world views are based. The motifs and themes within an Inuit creation story or the story of Pythagoras speak as much to their respective historic and cultural contexts as they speak to the context, shared among all peoples, of our common humanity. The stories attempt to shed light on many of the assumptions upon which you and I base our lives and give meaning to our worlds.

Specifically, I will propose that these stories are reflective of two very distinct value systems and ways of seeing the world, what I have come to term the *Looking Glass* and *Glass Pane* values. The Looking Glass (referring to a mirror) and Glass Pane (referring to a window) ways of seeing the world represent two of the most fundamental ways humanity has defined and continues to define itself. Both were found at the dawn of humanity. Both are found, though with varying emphasis, in virtually every community today. Both can even be found expressed by any given individual, you or me. But each is inherently distinct from the other. Each refers to contrasting ways of defining humanity and of relating to the world, of finding meaning and of enhancing well-being. The consequences of these two value configurations have far reaching implications for the quality of life for all in our contemporary world. I will

---

occurred in chronological time. An historical event is necessarily a past event. The "factuality" of history is to be appreciated and is expressed empirically as opposed to metaphorically and anagogically. Nevertheless, like myth, history can offer exemplary meaning; lessons are to be learned.

outline my own interpretation of the Looking Glass and Glass Pane values in the Epilogue section of this workbook.

In selecting the particular story texts included here, I have thus offered discussion on several basic questions revolving around our values and world views. Among them are how do the forms of the stories we tell, e.g., mythic or historic, influence how we relate to the world? How do our definitions of "person," of animal and plant, and of the world influence our relationship with the world? Specifically, how do our definitions of "wild" and of "domestic" "persons," be they animal, plant or human, influence our relations with the world? And then, what are the "rights" of those "persons"? In turn, what are our ethical responsibilities toward those "persons"? How do our understandings of our origin, our creation, influence our relations with the world? What are our criteria for what is knowable? In turn, how do our definitions and ways of acquiring knowledge influence our relationships with the world? What are our primary motivations and aspirations, and how do they affect our relations with the world about us? What are our greatest fears, and their consequences? What is it to be a "rich man," and what are its consequences for others, be they human, plant or animal? And what is wilderness? While this workbook can frame and pose such questions, their answers can only be suggested by those who engage its stories.

* * * * *

As with any endeavor that seeks to represent and communicate a text, this workbook is made up of a *deliberately* selected assemblage of texts. Only certain stories were included. Furthermore, the story texts are presented in a *particular manner* and *style*. A particular assemblage of words was used. While my intention is to offer descriptive story texts, unblemished by bias, I acknowledge that something of myself, the describer, is within the story texts. In the very act of selecting only certain story texts and then selecting particular words to describe those texts, an interpretation has necessarily been made. The narrative texts and the illustrations in this workbook were originally part of presentations and lectures I had made in various class sessions and, in turn, themselves based upon particular artistic, ethnographic or historic sources, each of which is identified in the story text. As will be suggested when we turn to a discussion of methodology in the next chapter, any attempt at presenting a cluster of symbols, such as these story texts, involves a synthesis of what is to be described and who is describing. I can only hope that my descriptions approximate, in some close fashion, the intended meanings of the original story texts, from which they were inspired and which they now represent.

* * * * *

The Looking Glass and Glass Pane values represent *contrasting* ways of defining humanity and relating to the world. Certainly other value orientations could have been considered. But it is in the contradistinction of the Looking Glass and Glass Pane stories that we can facilitate our primary intention in this workbook--that of *clarifying* and *interpreting values.* Let me elaborate our intentions.

FIRST, in offering these contrasting sets of stories, we will have an opportunity to explore and interpret the values of culturally distinct others and to gain an appreciation for the Looking Glass and Glass Pane ways of seeing the world. By gaining an appreciation for the different as presented in this workbook, an enhanced appreciation of and respect for the culturally "different" outside this workbook can also be gained. To communicate, to render services, and to cooperate with those of differing values, an appreciation and understanding of their perspective is an essential first step. In our ethnically diverse and culturally pluralistic world it is critical that we develop a tolerance of and respect for the varied world views of others. The vitality and integrity of our own society, and our ability to effectively function in our global community are directly related to the respect we give those with divergent points of view. With an appreciation of peoples who are culturally and ethnically distinct from ourselves we also acquire the best means to thwart the seeds of intolerance, prejudice and oppression.

SECOND, by offering an assemblage of varied stories, we will also have an opportunity to explore values closer to home, helping to reveal our own cultural and personal values. Despite their tremendous importance, we nevertheless seldom fully comprehend, no less articulate, our values. By juxtaposing that which is overtly distinct and distant along side that which is immediate but often veiled and elusive, the configuration of our own story and values become that much clearer. Or put another way, in "trying on" another's story, the uneasiness of the rub or the comfort of the fit help clarify the shape of our own contours.

To effectively communicate and cooperate with those of differing values and to gain a respect for culturally-different others, we must know our own values. To appreciate another, we must also come to appreciate ourselves.

In knowing our own stories and values, we also become cognizant of, deliberate in and ultimately more accountable for our own actions. We become the owners of our cultural values, and not owned by them. And thus in the revealing of our own values we can better celebrate or critically re-evaluate our stories and become accountable for them.

And THIRD, in offering a diverse assemblage of stories, we will have an opportunity to enhance our skills in critical thinking. Critical thinking involves the processes of revealing assumptions and exploring alternatives, and of making evaluations and formulating decisions. By glimpsing the breadth of the human experience, in all its rich diversity and in all its vast history, we are not only better able to appreciate our shared cultural foundations, but also challenge those false assumptions which are based upon a limited scope of our human existence. For instance, only after the human experience in its entirety is first appreciated is one in a better position to state, "it's only human nature" or "we're born that way." Far too often we postulate an "innate condition" as an "excuse" for a certain behavior, and in so doing, greatly inhibit the possibility of ever changing that condition and behavior.

In order to successfully approach this workbook and, I would suggest, life outside this workbook, we need to freely imagine and draw upon a full range of diverse and alternative perspectives and choices, as well as refuse to be bounded by narrowly defined and idiosyncratic view points. With an awareness of our own values and an appreciation of differing perspectives, we can better formulate and apply criteria for discriminating and evaluating life's varied experiential dilemmas.

* * * * *

I have selected the concept of "wilderness" as the reference point for our values clarification. Some expression or implication of "wilderness" will be evident in each of the story texts of this workbook. "Wilderness" is one of those concepts that goes to the very heart of how we, as a humanity, define and relate to the world about us. Yet, in turn, it is a concept not easily defined. There is no consensus. In fact that which is considered "wilderness" has galvanized considerable discussion and debate, both pro and con, by those who advocate for "wilderness areas" and those who oppose such designations. The concept resonates with emotional conviction; it is certainly value laden. This subjectivity is in part a function of how we use the word. While the term "wilderness" is itself a noun, we most often use it as an adjective, designating a certain quality, a "ness." There are "wilderness areas." You can have a "wilderness experience." Because of its elusive and subjective character, and yet because of its pivotal role in revealing how we in so many different ways relate to our world, the concept of "wilderness" is particularly well suited for our exercise in clarifying and interpreting values.

This workbook will thus be made up of a series of contrasting and richly textured story texts, stories within which are embedded the values that have defined our humanity, stories with which you will have an opportunity to eye juggle.

Song: A Methodology

Before you can begin your eye juggling, you must learn the old man's song and equip yourself with the language and method of eye juggling. The difficulty in comparing and attempting to understand an assortment of varied stories and contrasting value systems is in formulating and applying a methodology that does not compromise and distort the integrity of that which we seek to describe and understand. Too often the language we use to describe what is other than our own only clothes the other in the familiar. Eye juggling involves an appreciation of *symbols* and *values*, and the application of *interviewing* and *interpreting* skills. Together, they provide a method for better clarifying and appreciating the values of others as well as your own values.

Symbols

We had just come out of the downpour as we sped south on the Interstate Highway. Except for the sun's radiance from the west, the sky remained dark blue. Then we saw it, bright and clear, not more than a quarter mile to the east. With all its vivid colors, the rainbow emerged from the ground, arced and re-entered. It was a perfect rainbow.

But the perfect rainbow had something special to offer that afternoon. As we continued south, the rainbow seemed to move with us. We passed a wooded area, then a deep coulee, now a ranch house; at each site the rainbow touched down and moved across. We slowed the car to sneak a picture with the camera; the arc of color slowed as well. We sped up; it sped up. A hill

13

rose a few hundred feet from the car; the rainbow touched down so close that we could almost run our fingers through its vibrant colors.

We soon realized that this was our own rainbow. No one else would see it as we saw it. Others who traveled that road may also have seen a rainbow, even at the very same moment we saw ours, but theirs was not ours. It was a gift to us alone. And we gave thanks to the Rainbow.

* * * * *

A symbol can be defined as a specific *unit of reference* that refers to a particular *referent*. The unit of reference can be an object, a behavior, or a sign. The referent can consist of a concept, phenomenon or process. Simply put, a symbol is something that stands for something else.

In the story of the Rainbow, the word "rainbow" is the unit of reference that refers to an arc of vivid colors, a phenomenon, the referent. In the Eye Juggler story, the referents are concepts rather than phenomena, and are thus much more abstract and open to interpretation. "Look in the four directions and only the four," and "never try to see too much" are certainly units of reference expressed in explicit words. We can further isolate the images of behaviors such as "eyes as easily at home in the tree as in the head" or "eyes becoming stuck on the top branch and forever lost" as units of reference. Taken together, these units of reference may refer to the concept of "living in balance and not in greed with the world," the referent.

To enhance your understanding of symbols and your interpretative skills as an eye juggler, five critical dimensions of the symbol need to be briefly discussed.

FIRST, symbols presuppose *displacement*. The unit of reference refers to something that is separate from the temporal and spatial immediacy of the person who is symbolizing. The word "rainbow" can refer to something separate from the direct experience of seeing a rainbow. While you may have an image of that something in your mind, that image is not dependent on you directly experiencing it as you refer to it. The implications are far reaching. As a consequence of displacement, the human is forever free from the constraints of what is experienced and defined in the immediate and can contemplate distant places and times to create an endless inventory of images and meanings. And as I will suggest in the Epilogue, the human also is forever estranged and set apart from the natural world as a result of displacement.

SECOND, symbols entail *meaning*. Attached to any symbol is significance. The meaning associated with "rainbow" might be the anticipation of good fortune or the possibility of finding "a pot of gold" or simply the understanding of the colors of the spectrum formed by the refraction of the sun's rays on raindrops. While displacement allows the human to expand beyond the immediate, the meaning attached to symbols gives a significance to that expanded world. You may never have experienced eye juggling for yourself, but you may have an understanding of its meaning as the result of the Eye Juggler story. The meaningful world is thus limited only by what the human can imagine. As an eye juggler, it will be your challenge to discover the meaning embedded in the various story texts presented in this workbook.

THIRD, symbols can be transmitted in time and through space, i.e., they can be *learned* and *shared*. You may never have experienced eye juggling, but you have now learned something about it. The eye juggling may have occurred long ago, but you can know it in the present. The individual human is not limited to the sum total of his or her direct and idiosyncratic experiences, but is potentially able to be inclusive of the collective experiences of an entire human society and history. As eye jugglers and with great interpretative skills, we can gain access to much of the meaning of world views quite distinct from our own; all because symbols can be shared and learned.

FOURTH, the meaning attached to the symbol is autonomous of and not bound by the unit of reference, i.e., any given symbol can refer to anything. The meaning of a symbol is *arbitrary*. The word "rainbow" can refer to the anticipation of good luck or it can refer to evil and the devil or, for some, the word may have absolutely no meaning at all. There is nothing innate within the unit of reference that would necessitate and bind the word "rainbow" to a certain meaning. It is this quality of arbitrariness that distinguishes a symbol from a sign. The meaning associated with a sign is tightly bound to its unit of reference. For instance, to cup one's hands and draw them to one's mouth is a unit of reference indicative of drinking or thirst. But, as a symbol, the word "cup" can refer to a container or possibly to the act of drinking or to a virtually endless assortment of meanings.

As a function of this arbitrariness, any given symbol can have an assortment of differing meanings and that assortment can occur simultaneously. Further, the processes of creativity and imagination are made possible. New, never before conceived of meanings can be brought forth, e.g., eye juggling! With the spontaneity of creativity and imagination, language is rendered "open-ended."

But also because of this arbitrariness, the interpretation of story texts is made that much more difficult. The meanings of symbols, especially symbols originating out of world views different from our own, are never overt nor explicit and are always open to misinterpretation.

FIFTH, symbols define the parameters of and assign the meaning to the phenomenal world of objects and of images, i.e., that which symbols refer to is *brought forth* and *created*. The meaning of an object or image does not rest in that object or image alone, but is the result of a complex interaction involving the object or image, human sensory perception, and human mental conception. Conceptualization, in turn, is influenced by the particular cultural and historical paradigms of the specific human who is conceptualizing.

What is it that constitutes the phenomenon, "rainbow"? Certainly the mist of the rain and the light of the sun are critical elements. But a certain interaction is also necessary. The light must refract off the mist. And do we not also need a human perceiving of that particular interaction of light and mist? Would a "rainbow" exist without a human physically seeing it, and seeing it in only a particular relationship and angle to the light and mist? And do we not also need a human conceiving of that particular interaction? Would a "rainbow" exist without a concept of it, without a symbol rendering it a meaningful phenomenon, assigning a particular significance to it? The "rainbow" was recognized, "as we sped south on the Interstate Highway," and assigned a particular significance, "our own rainbow," "a gift to us alone" and "we gave thanks to the Rainbow," rendering that phenomenon meaningful.

This is not to suggest that there is nothing unless it is symbolized. While lacking a particular symbol for "wall," the physicality of a wall still has an abrupt existence when encountered. While clouded in considerable mystery, a spiritual archetype is not denied because it lacks a particular icon. It is simply not revealed. And most assuredly the light and the mist, and the experiencing of them has an existence, is something. But that "something" is fundamentally meaningless. If there is not a particular symbol of that phenomenon, for example, "rainbow," can that phenomenon have meaning? Thus typically and most importantly, that which is not symbolized is *not readily recognized* and is *not given meaning* by the human.

While symbols define and, in a sense, limit how we relate to the world by establishing parameters of meaning, symbols also remove cognitive barriers and expand the realm of possible human experience. If a new symbol is brought forth, is not a new meaningful phenomenon also brought forth? Because of their arbitrary, autonomous character, symbols can create new and varied ways of rendering meaning and experiencing the world.

Let me offer as an illustration the symbol "wilderness." What you consider as "wilderness" has a specific range of meanings, which defines how you relate to that which you signify by this symbol. For example, "wilderness" may be understood as a pristine, natural area, not to be tampered with by humanity. Therefore, it may be difficult for you to imagine other ways of relating to that which you signify as "wilderness" phenomenon. But that difficulty does not preclude the possibility of other people assigning altogether different meanings to the symbol, "wilderness." For example, "wilderness" can be understood as a vast natural resource, to be used to satisfy human economic needs. And of course the difficulty in imagining other ways of relating to this phenomenon also does not preclude the possibility of altogether new meanings being created and assigned to the symbol. For example, "wilderness" might be thought of as the chaos found in the inner city. As with any symbol, "wilderness" has a multiplicity of possible meanings, any and all of which you have an ability to learn from another person or to create anew for yourself. These newly established meanings are thus incorporated into your understanding and usage of the symbol "wilderness." Subsequently, you would probably relate and act in new ways to that which you refer to as "wilderness." For example, now the possibility exists, however unlikely, that instead of going into an Alpine meadow or an "old-growth forest," you would venture into an "inner city" to receive a "wilderness experience!" That which is "wilderness" takes on new meanings and is related to in new ways. Any symbol can therefore at once limit yet expand how you relate to the world.

Symbols ultimately liberate the human from the temporal and spatial constraints imposed by the immediacy of existence, and allow humans to live in an expanded world of their own fabrication and imagination.

From the most minute and seemingly insignificant to the most grandiose and pervasive, all of human thought, activity, and expression are invariably symbolic. A glance of the eye or the spatial proximity with another person, the particular clothing worn, the numbers of a mathematician, the images of an artist, the design of a building, the spoken word, the written word, the stories you are about to read: all are clustering of symbols. Humanity is *homo symbolicus*.

Values

The particular cluster of symbols that is of concern to us is values. In your eye juggling, it will be the values embedded within the story texts that you will attempt to discover and interpret. I will define values as *learned, relatively enduring, emotionally charged, epistemologically grounded and represented moral conceptualizations that assist us in making judgements and in preparing us to act.* In other words, the priorities we set and the choices we make are significantly based upon the values we hold. My usage of the concept is inclusive of the personal values of an individual as well as the collective values of a community.

All values are *learned* values. Not unlike the acquisition of a particular language, values are transmitted and inculcated through an intricate web of societal agents and interactions. Primary to this web are family members and social peers, formal schooling, leisure, work and religious activities, and such rites of passage as baptism, confirmation and marriage. And interwoven throughout this web is the oral and/or written word, the stories of a people. The influence of this web is particularly important during childhood when the basic value parameters are established. In turn, these parameters help orient the subsequent acquisition and the reaffirmation of values throughout a person's life-span.

Because values are learned, they can be forgotten, and they can be learned anew, though usually only with great effort. But values can be changed. Humanity is neither innately predisposed to certain values; nor is the content of values genetically determined.[1]

---

[1]My concern here is not to suggest how an individual forms his or her particular values. Furthermore, these comments are not meant to preclude the insights of such theorists as Noam Chomsky, Erik Erikson or Jean Piaget. The possibility that humans have certain biologically-based maturation levels and predispositions influencing the acquisition of language and personality must be considered in any discussion of the acquisition of values. Suffice it to say, the formation of an individual's

Values are relatively *enduring*. Values are grounded in the cultural heritage of a society and pervasively housed within the institutions of the society, the web.   And values are well established from childhood.   An individual may decide to forego a particular value, only to be confronted by it at each juncture within the web of society and to be grounded by its parameters formed early in life. The values of a society or of an individual are not easily altered.

Values are *not* necessarily *consciously* known by either the individual or the society.   Not unlike our everyday linguistic grammar, values are seldom overtly articulated, even though we depend upon both in comprehending another's action and in generating our own.   Your search for your own values and the values of others is accomplished only with great effort.

Values tend toward *consistency*, i.e., like values attract like values. The assemblage of an individual's or of a community's values strives for affiliation, compatibility and integration among those values.   If a particular value is not consistent with the assemblage of values already held, it is not easily integrated and is often ignored and excluded.

This is not to suggest that we will always find consistency among the values held by any given individual or expressed in a given community. Values *strive* for consistency. The particular assemblage of values of an individual or community is typically inclusive of disparate and often mutually contradictory values. It may even be the case that a particular configuration of values not only accommodates but espouses seemingly contradictory values.   At issue is not the inconsistent disposition of the individual values in question, but the overall structure of the relationships and the character of that integration among all those values. To understand any given value, one must also consider the larger gestalt in which it is embedded. Such a contradiction will be observed when we discuss the Crow Indian values of oneness and unity, and differentiation and uniqueness.   The

---

value configuration is an extremely complex process.

apparent inconsistency is dissolved when the specific contextual integration, in this instance, the imagery of the "circle" and "wagon wheel," is taken into consideration.

Values enshrine and impart a society's concepts of the *morally desirable*. Values set forth the social criteria for and the cultural assumptions upon which good and bad, right and wrong, moral and immoral, noble and vile are established. Values provide a code and form the basis for all moral judgments, whether directed at others, nature or the self. Values guide human conduct, providing a "road map" for action. Of course, what one may value as proper, another may value as immoral and improper. As a consequence, values are often at the focal point of conflict.

Values are inundated with *emotional* feelings and are held with strong conviction. There can be no passively neutral values. Fear, sympathy, hate, love, anger, passion, contempt: all are expressions of this subjective dimension of values. Values are most assuredly felt.

Because of this affective component, values are thus more than a code of conduct. By infusing judgements with passion, values establish the desirable. Good and bad are not simply laid out; "good" is passionately desired and "bad" is ardently avoided. Values are the great *motivators* within a society and the individual; the drive directed toward all sorts of ends. From how a "rich man" is defined to what is most "feared" in life: all are grounded in values. But it is also this passion that certainly can inhibit an appreciation of values different from one's own. Emotions can cloud a clear vision.

Values establish a *disposition to act*. Values influence our behaviors by preparing us to act in certain morally-oriented ways. When a certain behavioral response is called for in a given context of social interaction, what that behavior may be is based in part upon the values held. I suggest "in part" because values, while primary among those influences, are not the sole influence on our behaviors. Other influences include the level of individual self-esteem, social role definitions, societal laws, spontaneous collective behavior and the persuasiveness of others, for instance. Consequently, identified values alone are not necessarily accurate predictors of behavior. While they closely parallel one another, the values we hold and the behaviors we exhibit are not the reverse sides of the same coin, each synonymous with the other.

Any given value is based upon and expressed in terms of certain *epistemological criteria*. Upon what standard of knowing is a particular value acknowledged and represented? How is a particular value validated by the holder of that value? In what terms is a value framed and publicly presented? To assert, for example, that "wilderness is a vast, as yet untapped natural resource to be harvested" implies a value based upon and expressed in terms of epistemological criteria that is "economic" in nature. "Wilderness" is *known* in terms of a "commodity" that has "production value," and that can be distributed and consumed.

While there is a range of possible epistemological criteria on which values can be grounded, for our interpretative purposes, only three will be isolated: literal-denotative, metaphoric-connotative, and anagogic-implicative.[2] These categories are not mutually exclusive. Any given value can be based on more than one of these criteria simultaneously, e.g., literal-denotative and anagogic-implicative. Furthermore, each category has validity, equally contributing to the human condition, although in differing ways. No one criteria, in and of itself, is more appropriate or morally superior than another. This is not a developmental sequence through which an individual progresses from one stage to the next.

Literal-denotative values are those which are promulgated on the *physical senses* and have *explicit*, literal meanings. The types of senses on which these values are based are those overtly acknowledged as viable and generally shared among a given group, e.g., sight and sound. These values are understood to be

---

[2]This typology owes much to the writings of Ananda Coomaraswamy 1934.

grounded on and have legitimacy because of something that has a reality in the experiential world.

Let me offer two examples of literal-denotative value statements that focus on "wilderness." "Wilderness is made up of a given number and type of trees, animals, plants, in a specified physical terrain." As referred to in the Old Testament, wilderness is a "desert" and "waste," a "cursed" land, full of "thorns and thistles." In both instances, the value statements are based on literal meanings, accessible through the senses. You can touch the trees and feel the thorns. The words descriptive of "wilderness" attempt to elicit precise, literal representations. The word "tree" has a more or less precise physical counterpart in the "wilderness." Empiricism and religious fundamentalism, for example, are associated with literal-denotative values.

Metaphoric-connotative values are those based on mental *conceptualization* and have *implicit*, metaphoric meanings. These values can range from the logically oriented, i.e., based on a consensus of shared rules for thinking, to the irrationally focused, i.e., formed without a consensus of shared rules for thinking and based upon fallacious assumptions. They are often predicated on and are legitimized because of a deduction from or a comparison to other values. They are not dependent upon being grounded in the experiential world. Metaphoric-connotative value statements offer more figurative and abstract images, often images of qualities, and are much less literal in their representations.

Let me illustrate this type of value with three different examples. "Wilderness is the antithesis of civilization." "Wilderness is a land of no use." "Wilderness is where the birds fly free and the beauty of the flowers glows with the colors of the rainbow." These particular wilderness value statements are deduced from and implicitly compared with other already held values, i.e., values of societal civilization, economic use and aesthetic beauty. They have little direct and no literal counterpart in an experiential "wilderness," but refer to images of abstract qualities. Rationalism, literary criticism and racial prejudice, for example, are all founded on metaphoric-connotative values.

Anagogic-implicative values are those which are derived from *intuitive* or *mystical* experiences and have *implicit*, metaphoric meanings. It is often the meaning of the "essence" within something overt and material, the "inner forms." While emanating out of and legitimized by an experience, unlike literal-denotative values, that experience is much more private and contemplative in nature, e.g., divine revelation, and not contingent upon certain senses that are generally shared by all in the community. Although this is not to suggest that in any given community all members could not have access to such an experience. Similar to metaphoric-connotative values, anagogic-implicative value statements offer figurative, abstract images, and meanings. But these are images that are normally hidden from humanity and often esoteric in nature, e.g., the image of an animal's soul.

An example of an anagogic-implicative value statement would be, "Wilderness is where God and all true wisdom are to be found." Another example would be, "The image in the stone is that of the seal, revealed through the stone by the seal to the stone carver as he sat in the great solitudes." Both statements offer figurative meanings, i.e., images of God and of a seal-spirit, and are derived from a mystical or intuitive ways of knowing. Anagogic-implicative values are not dependent upon empirical or logical processes. Artistic and religious inspiration, for example, are associated with anagogic-implicative values.

The ingrained values expressed throughout our stories form much of the basis for who and what we are. They help us to interpret and comprehend the behaviors of others as well as to guide our own behaviors through the mazeway of human existence.

Interviewing

To enhance your skills in appreciating the values of another person, eye juggling involves your ability to go beyond the story texts of this workbook. You will be asked to conduct an interview of someone's life history or his or her oral traditions, and then to assemble that information as a "story text," as a "cultural story." In so doing, you will have a wonderful opportunity to come close to truly experiencing the richness and depth of meaning in the story of another human being. As with all our eye juggling endeavors, the overriding concern is to seek out, in the interview questions, and to convey, in the subsequent written narrative, the story *from the perspective* of the person interviewed.

Your first task will be to select someone to interview. Try to select an *interviewee* whose values are distinct from your own. It is much easier to come to understand a story whose territory is distinct from one's own. Perhaps the individual is of another ethic or cultural group. Perhaps there is simply an occupational or generational difference. Most of all, select someone who sincerely wants to share his or her story with you. In selecting someone to interview, you should not need to go beyond the members of your own local community. Wonderful stories are always to be found close to home.

Before you begin the actual interview, think about the information you hope to gather. What are the goals of your project? What sort of information are you seeking? Is it a *life history* of a particular individual (first-person, idiosyncratic experiences, i.e., "he/she did it", bound by a specific cultural and historical context)? Is it the *oral traditions* of another person that you seek (stories, traditions, historical information passed down through different people to your interviewee, remembrances not necessarily experienced by the interviewee, "he/she learned it from others")? Or is it possibly a person's *mythology* ("true stories" which are expressive of universal motifs and archetypes, and are considered "timeless")? What are the particular parameters of your research, e.g., a particular geographic area, historical period, economic way of life, educational or health care system, or governmental or religious structure? Who might best be able to offer you the information you seek? Is your interviewee a "willing" and enthusiastic participant? Does he/she have the time to work with you?

Goal setting is the single most important aspect of your project. Ask yourself where you are at now, where do you want to go and how are you going to get there? Clarify your goals and your means to get there. Fuzzy goals result in frustration and missing important information. Have a vision of what may await you, but also be willing to re-direct your goals as you grow in your project. Develop a list of potential interviewees. Make a topical outline, establishing your research parameters and goals.

Don't go into the interview "cold." Gain an awareness of the cultural context and historical background of the particular information you seek. Research your topics. Consult with relatives and friends of your intended interviewee, local historians, libraries, newspapers, university resources. Learn the broad characteristics of the territory. What sorts of questions need to be asked?

Prepare *open-ended questions*. You may know the broad topics, but you do not know the specifics. You're as an "infant," learning someone else's cultural story for the first time. "You don't know it." Use open-ended, evocative questions like: "Why did you...?" "How did you feel about...?" "What was it like...?" "Could you describe how...?" "What sort of person was he/she...?" Ask the who, what, when and most importantly, the why questions. Open-ended questions let your interviewee set the direction of information sharing and let him/her "lead." Ask questions that spark the imagination and focus the interview, that attempt to reveal the cultural story of the interviewee.

If you are seeking a person's life history, develop questions that chronicle a life-span, questions about birth place, parents and family, memories from infancy and adolescents, schooling, travel, employment, etc.

Avoid closed-ended questions that elicit "yes-no" answers like: "Did you like...?" "Were you affected by your teachers ...?" "Are the traditions still...?" They have their place, such as determining the date and place of birth, years in school, etc. But it is a limited place.

Avoid generalities like: "Tell me all about your childhood...?" which elicits nothing more than a list of names and dates, and a very bored interviewee. Ask instead, "What did you like to do when you were six or seven?"

Write down your questions. Know the questions you seek from your interviewee. But don't be rigid about your list. Questions will always be waiting for you once you are in the actual interview process.

To get shy people to open up to the interview, take along photos or objects (heirlooms or memorabilia, tools, maps, diagrams, etc.) and ask the interviewee to tell you about them. Props can also "draw out memories." Remember to number each prop and mention it in the tape recording.

In order to accurately record and, in turn, communicate another's cultural story, it is recommended that you use an audio or video *tape recorder*. It is preferable that your recorder has a detachable microphone in order to pick-up the best possible sound quality. Be familiar with your taping equipment. Experiment with mike placement, volume, brand of tape, etc. before you begin. Make sure the sound quality is good. Gather recording equipment: video recorder and tripod or audio cassette recorder, blank tapes (unwrap tapes, advance lead of tape and always bring more blank tapes than you think you'll need), fresh batteries or extension cord and 3-prong adaptor, separate microphone and foam pad, pen and note pad.

It is critical that you first gain *permission* from your interviewee to use the obtained information. If someone else's cultural story is to be shared publicly (with fellow students or placed in a library archive, for example), a copyright release should be signed by the interviewee. See the attached Copyright Release Form in the Appendix.

In addition to oral interview information, do not forget to gather other cultural artifacts such as family photographs, art work, etc. Copies may have to be made from them. As you collect these objects be sure to catalog them and record all information known about them.

To get started with the interview, make an appointment with your interviewee ahead of time (in person, phone or letter). Be sure that the location for the interview is at a site that minimizes interference by others. Be on time to your first interview session. Schedule the session around the interviewee's family needs. Clearly introduce yourself and your project intentions to your interviewee. Answer any questions about the project. Go over the Copyright Release Form and gain his or her signature. Clearly explain the procedures, and the focus and parameters of the interview. Interview only one person at a time. If you're talking to the interviewee and another person wants to put in his "two cents' worth," tell him you would love to interview him, but at another time soon. It's best to make this clear before you begin your interview. The best way to guarantee this is to have just you and your interviewee present in the room. Make sure there's no background noise (t.v., dishwasher, other conversations) that may interfere with the quality of the tape. Make sure everyone is comfortable, with good seating and water. And always do a brief test of your audio/video equipment to be sure the mike is picking up both voices clearly.

Break the ice by chatting briefly about related topics before you start the tape recording. But don't turn the tape recorder off and on more then absolutely necessary once it's going. It's a good idea to tape a brief introductory lead-in before you ask your first question. Tell who is being interviewed, by whom, when, and the general subjects to be covered.

A key to a successful interview is in using good questioning and listening skills. Be honest and sincere, "be yourself." Interviewing is the art form of dialoguing with another human being; you are in conversation with someone else. It is a give-and-take situation. If you want honest and sincere information, you have to give it. Get acquainted. Establish your "kinship;" establish "*rapport*."

Begin by asking for a brief (2 or 3 minute) bit of background information about the interviewee: where and when born, parents, major places lived during life, careers or other important areas of personal experiences.   Easy to answer and non-intimidating questions help relax the interviewee.

People can usually describe concrete things more easily than conceptual.   Start with the concrete.   You want answers that are descriptive as well as factual.   "Can you describe your home outside and inside?" or "Would you explain to me what you did in a typical day's work?" are good examples.

Don't talk too much about yourself.   Resist the impulse to contribute your own stories or information or to put words in the mouth of the person you're interviewing.

Don't talk to the recorder or the mike; talk to the person you're interviewing, with lots of direct eye contact (if appropriate, given the cultural considerations of your interviewee).   If you act as if the mike isn't there, chances are your interviewee will soon forget about it, too.

Refer now and then to your general topical questions; keep your goals in mind.   But don't let your specific questions and goals become your "script."   Let the interviewee set the direction and the lead; he/she is the one with the information.   Be an *active listener*.   Ask questions based upon your interviewee's responses.   Be flexible.   Don't be afraid of going off on a "tangent."   Don't be so anxious about asking your next question that you fail to hear what your interviewee is saying.

Sometimes the best information comes up unexpectedly.   If you're into something good, follow it up with appropriate, *follow-up questions*.   Follow-up questions can also elicit more detailed information as well as to make sure your interviewee has had a chance to tell all he/she wants to tell.   "What happened then?" "How did you feel about that?"   "How did that turn out?"   After pursuing this line of inquiry, guide the interviewee back to your original questions.

Try not to interrupt your interviewee.   If your interviewee mentions something you'd like to follow up, wait for a natural pause in the conversation and then say something like: "A few minutes ago you were saying that..."   Don't ask more than one question at a time.

Don't rush into every pause with a new question. Silences are natural, and they may give your interviewee a chance to think of additional materials on the subject. Silence is not wasted time. Take advantage of the "*silent probe*."

Show your interviewee that you're interested through nods and facial expressions. Express your appreciation with occasional responses like: "That's a great story!" or "That's really interesting!" The way you ask questions, your tone of voice, your body language, are all keys to the responses your questions will get.

Don't make irrelevant or distracting comments. And never contradict your interviewee, whether you agree with what the person is saying or not. Instead, ask further questions that shed light on the issue being discussed. It may help you determine the various versions to a given situation or event. There can be many differing accounts of the same event, all of which are "correct." Remember the difference between interviewing and cross-examining.

If your interviewee can't or won't give you an answer to a particular question, it's better to move on. You must acknowledge that there will be some information that you will not be able to gather. Gaps will exist. Some of the story may not be meant to be shared publicly. It may be too personal or even sacred for your interviewee.

Establish a basic time frame by asking: "What year was that?" or "About how old were you when that happened?" If your interviewee doesn't know, try to get at least a rough idea by asking a further question like: "How long afterward was that, a month? a year?"

Try to establish what your interviewee's role was in the events he/she is describing--a participant, an observer, etc. Or, if he/she is passing on a story rather than describing a personal experience, try to determine who he/she heard it from or the original source of the story.

If your interviewee uses unusual words or linguistic terms that are unfamiliar to you, have the interviewee explain them and try to spell them out.

Adjust the length of the interview to your interviewee's comfort and attention span. Forty-five minutes to an hour is a good length. If it's too short it will probably be superficial, and if it's too long it will get uncomfortable. You can always take a break and resume later. Older folks tire more easily; cut the interview off at the first sign of fatigue.

It is likely that numerous sessions will be needed for some interviewees. Let the interviewee know ahead of time that there can be future sessions.

And always remember whose story you're trying to tell. Try not biasing your information with your own perspective. You want to present the story of your interviewee from *his/her own perspective*. Attempt to see the world through his/her eyes. You have the tremendous responsibility of continuing to speak your interviewee's voice for all the others, as well as the future generations, who will read your interview.

After the interview is completed, show your sincere appreciation by *thanking* your interviewee. Then follow-up with a formal letter of appreciation. Ask your interviewee if he/she is willing to sign the Copyright Release Form (if he/she has not already done so), allowing you to share his or her story publicly.

Label the tape clearly with the name of your interviewee, the date and your name. Break out the tabs on the tape so it doesn't get erased by accident.

Indexing the interview is the next essential step. Prepare a written index of the audio/video tape recording, using a stopwatch or clock. The purpose of the index is to summarize the contents of the interview and to indicate approximately where on the tape a certain subject is discussed.

Indexing by the minute is best since the meter number systems vary from machine to machine. Use a stopwatch or a clock. Divide the tape into approximately five-minute segments or by the obvious breaks in subjects.

Make your index fairly detailed--especially if you do not intend to transcribe the entire taped interview. A detailed index will make even a cassette that is not transcribed useful to other researchers. Index by names, dates, place names, processes, family names, customs, events, etc., indicated by the information in the interview. Do the index as soon as possible after the interview so the subjects are still fresh in your mind.

Using the index of the tape recording as your guide, next *transcribe* those selected portions of the text that you want to include in your written report. The goal in transcribing an interview is to provide an accurate, verbatim written record of the interview dialogue in a form which will best represent your interviewee's cultural story. Transcribe everything that is said by the interviewee, including colloquial pronunciations, "yeah" and "goin'," as well as indicate the pauses in the speech pattern, phrase repetitions, and voice inflections placed on specific words. Meaning is conveyed not only in the words spoken but also in the way those words are spoken.

There is an acknowledged relationship between *what* you present and *how* you present it. Given the nature of your information, be it oral history/life history or be it mythology, the style of presentation can enhance or detract from the intended meaning of the cultural story. For example, if you include mythological stories, should you not also include a copy of an audio presentation of that story by the narrator as part of the report? The form and style of your finished product should be dictated by the type of information you collect.

It is strongly recommended that you show your written index and the story transcription to your interviewee and ask him/her to check it for accuracy. After all, your interviewee is the "authority." A review can also spark additional insights and memories by the interviewee. Be ready for another interview session.

It is most appropriate to leave a copy of the transcribed story text with your interviewee. There is no better way of saying *thank you* than by presenting your interviewee with a personal copy of his or her own story. You may also want to donate the cultural story (tape, index and transcription) to your local library or college oral history achieve.

Interpreting

In the words of the famous American baseball player, Yogi Berra, "what gets us into trouble is not what we don't know, it's what we know for sure that just ain't so."

* * * * *

We are constantly presented with story texts, be they the stories in this workbook, the transcribed pages of a life history interview, or more typically in a passing conversation with someone in your community. How do you go about eye juggling a story text? How do you interpret the values embedded within someone's story?

As we had mentioned previously, if behavior is not a direct corollary of values, then you can not automatically observe values in someone's behavior and actions. And if values are not necessarily consciously articulated, then you can not readily ask someone what his or her values are and expect him or her to offer a concise treatise on them. Then how do you come to understand another person's values?

As we have established, values are clustering of symbols. As such, the symbolic is indicative of values. Values are found ingrained within such symbolic expressions as artistic forms, ceremonial rites, architectural structures, legal enactments, written history, written literature, and oral literature, all of which are story texts. Values are also to be found embedded in speech patterns and hand gestures, in clothing and even hair styles, in all the behavioral actions expressed, all of which are story texts. These are among the types of texts that will be the focus of your eye juggling.

It is somehow appropriate to point out that these texts are also the types of symbolic expressions, channeled through various societal institutions, that directly contribute to the acquisition and enculturation of any person's values. Much in the same manner in which another person acquires his or her values, so will you learn of those values.

The goal in interpreting the values of another is to see from the *perspective of the other*, to eye juggle with the eyes of the storyteller within the story, and to avoid the indiscriminate imposition of your own perspective on that of the other, to avoid being biased and *ethnocentric*. This is a challenge accomplished only with great diligence. To view the story texts from the inside out, several basic interpretative techniques can be applied.

The folklorist Alan Dundes points the way in our interpretation of stories.[3] For Dundes, interpretation involves the clarification of the text, the texture and the context of the story. The *text* refers to the symbolic meanings of the actual text, e.g., what is being said, what are the world view themes or moral lessons of the story, what is referred to by the key symbols? The *texture* refers to how the text is being presented, e.g., what is the style of the writing or the techniques of the telling, what are the interactions with the readers or the listeners, what are the linguistic components and structures, such as particular phonemes and morphemes, intonation and pitch, pause duration, and phrase repetitions? How something is stated affects what something means. The *context* refers to when and where the text is being presented, e.g., to whom, when, where, in what social situation and for what cultural purpose is the story directed? A comprehension of the context requires development of an understanding of the entire cultural configuration in which the story is embedded.

The suggested interpretative techniques which follow are predicated on the distinctions between the text, texture and context of a story. They should be applied to the interpretation of the story texts as found in this workbook, in the life history interview you just completed, or in that conversation you had with your next door neighbor.

As you approach a story text, first read it for "pleasure" and then read it for "study." Your initial reading should not be

---

[3]See Dundes 1966.

particularly analytical, but rather an attempt to imagine yourself within the story, as one of the characters. Listen for the voice of the "storyteller" within the story. *Familiarize* yourself with the landscape of the story. Then re-read the text, this time more thoroughly and carefully, paying attention to both the details as well as to the "big picture."

Throughout the entire interpretative process, apply our definitions of "symbol" and "value." Attempt to isolate the key symbols within the text of the story. They will help point the way to the underlying values of the text. Ask yourself what meanings and images are being referred to in each individual phrase and passage. Who are the central characters of the text? How would you characterize their actions? Are there any lessons to be learned from those actions?

Within any given text, you may find a variety of seemingly disparate units of reference that, in fact, refer to a singular, affiliated meaning or image. Often a related image will be reiterated throughout a text in a variety of ways in order to convey a specific meaning. Look for the repetitions.

Meaning is often context bound. Ask yourself how the referent meaning of a specific passage relates to the other images and meanings of the entire text. Attempt to see the gestalt of the text, not just the individual units of reference. What may be the larger implications of what is being referred to in the text? Ask yourself in what social context is the text usually presented. When and where is it likely to be found? To whom is it usually directed? Attempt to ground the text in its cultural and historical context.

Ask yourself what sort of epistemological criteria are alluded to in the text, i.e., literal-denotative, metaphoric-connotative and/or anagogic-implicative. Ask yourself what sort of story text and thus value system you have before you.

Observe and listen to the texture of the story text, that is, not only what is being said, but how it is said. Are you reading a written text, or listening to an oral narrative, or viewing an artistic image? How does each form of expression affect the meaning of the text? If it is an oral-based text, pay special attention to the contextual setting and the textural components, e.g., raconteur's intonation patterns or use of repetition.

As you approach a story text, you are in fact interpreting it on two distinct levels. Certainly focus on the story that is being portrayed, *what* the story is. But also consider the presentation of that story, *how* the story is conveyed and portrayed. For instance, in the "Dream Animal" text, a story of early human evolution and culture, you might identify as a value embedded within the story, "survival." A value motivating early humanity was its desire to physically survive in a harsh environment. But you might also interpret in the presentation of that story, the value of relying on the "physical facts." How the story of human evolution is presented is predicated on valuing empirical evidence. As you may then discover, there is often a correspondence between the two levels. *How* something is stated is inextricably related to *what* something means.

For those story texts which originally emanated out of an oral-based tradition, they should be accessed by first listening to them. Such texts are presented in this workbook in a "poetic style," and are to be found in "Soul Food," "A Flower," "The Quest," "Three Hots and a Cot," and "The Give-Away." Have another person read those particular sections aloud to you, paying attention to the pauses and word phrasing within those texts. An oral performance will help enunciate implicit meanings within certain types of story texts, while a written format and a subsequent reading of them is much more appropriate for interpreting other types of texts.

Most important of all to the interpretative process is to re-engage the story text a second time; leave the text for another activity; return to the text, reading it aloud this time. Dwell in the text. Gain some perspective; hear it in many voices. When all is said and done, to interpret is to soil the pages of the text. Interpretation is accomplished only after a *great labor*. And most telling, to interpret is to allow the words of the stories to be lifted from the pages of the text and for you, the interpreter, to dance with them. Listen for the words of the storyteller within the story. Interpretation necessitates an intimacy with the images and characters within the story text.

But even before you can begin dancing with the stories of others, you must know something of the stories within yourself. You must juggle your own eyes. To properly interpret another's values you need to be *aware of your own*; otherwise their values simply become extensions of your values as you inadvertently cloud your interpretation with your own values.

When life in the Mexican village of Tepoztlan was first described by the American anthropologist Robert Redfield (1930), it was a "folk life" characterized as cooperative and integrated, made up of content, well-adjusted people. When Oscar Lewis (1951) restudied the same village, tension, schism, pervading fear, envy and distrust characterized Tepoztlan. Had some twenty years brought so much change? Or had Redfield and Lewis, however unwittingly, each brought something of their respective cultural milieu into their studies? For Redfield, had it been the optimism of an age of prosperity in which "the War to end all wars" had just been fought and a League of Nations established? For Lewis, was it the tension and fear of an age of Cold War, the "Bomb" and global conflict?

This is not to suggest that you must somehow "empty" yourself and view from a "void" so as not to bias your interpretation. One can not see well without eyes accustomed to viewing. What is suggested is that you acknowledge and distinguish what is indeed your story from the story of the other. Your story should not become their story.

It may even be the case that the acknowledged qualities and perspectives of your own story may help assist you in revealing the meaning of another's story. Your own eyes (as well as the eyes of another) can offer insights. To have appreciated your own walk in the forest is to better appreciate the meaning of someone else's walk in a forest. To have appreciated your own story of divinity is to better appreciate the meaning of divinity in someone else's story.[4]

In 1930, the British anthropologist E. E. Evans-Pritchard initiated what would become the definitive study of the Nuer, an east African Nilotic people. The first in a series of works, *The Nuer: A description of the modes of livelihood and political institutions of a Nilotic people* (1940), quickly became a classic in the field. With the outbreak of World War II, Evans-Pritchard was forced to relinquish his research and return to England. While there, he became a Catholic. With the war concluded, Evans-Pritchard resumed his studies among the Nuer, and in 1956 published *Nuer Religion*. While describing the same people, albeit differing domains within the same culture, in comparing *The Nuer* with *Nuer Religion* it is as if two different writers were at work. In *The Nuer*, it was a humanity defined in terms of the praxis and functional qualities of its social existence. While in *Nuer Religion*, it was the symbolic and ideational qualities that defined this humanity. Was it his own newly acquired religious sensitivities that allowed Evans-Pritchard to gain access to and then to better appreciate Nuer spiritual sensibilities? And in the instances of Redfield and Lewis, could not the times from which each viewed the world have actually helped reveal differing aspects of the same village life in Tepoztlan? While you do not want to bias your interpretative endeavors, you should not abandon your values. When you have acknowledged your own values, the view through the lenses of those values can help reveal the values of others.

As previously mentioned, perhaps the most effective way to discover and acknowledge your own values is to juxtapose what is other and different along side what is immediate but often veiled. The contours of your own values will be made that much clearer. Read through the various story texts. Ask yourself how

---

[4]But of course, access to the meaning of another's story of a forest walk or of divinity is not contingent upon your possessing a comparable story. There would be very little interpreting and understanding of another's story if such were the case.

you feel about the various images presented and issues raised in those texts. Is there a sense of familiarity or is there an uneasy distance? Most importantly, ask *why* is there a familiarity or uneasiness? Which of your own values is subsequently being exposed? In traveling the unfamiliar territory of the other, the climate will quickly let you know if you are dressed properly. Observe what you are wearing.

If you are to interpret properly, you must thus be accountable for the values you bring into the interpretative precess. Attempt to minimize the unintentional clouding of your interpretations by the coloring of your own values. But also allow your own acknowledged values to assist in navigating the unknown territory of the other. And then try to clearly see that territory; try to see from the perspective of the other.

The goal of interpreting from the perspective of the other, however, is an *elusive goal*. In the final analysis, you can never fully know the meaning of someone else's values. Your interpretations are always *isomorphic*, i.e., an approximation of, but not identical with, that which you are interpreting. The interpretation of values can never be empirical. This should not discourage you from being rigorous in your endeavors, however. Your interpretations have tremendous *heuristic value*. They assist in discovery and exploration. They assist in arriving at more appropriate ways of learning about and describing the human condition. They assist in increasing your overall understanding and appreciation of yourself and others. Interpretation humanizes your experiences with others. Eye juggling is not a science; it is an art.

Interpretation is ultimately a process of *creating symbolic meanings*. As previously discussed, if something is not symbolized, it is not readily recognizable and has no meaning. If the interpreter does not have a symbol of the other, the other has no meaning. A new symbol is needed. As further discussed, if the meaning of the symbols of the other is elusive, you can not simply and automatically appropriate the symbols of the other. Simply presenting another's symbol does not mean you have presented the meaning of that symbol as understood by the other. A new symbol is needed. And if you impose your own symbols on the other, you only blind yourself from seeing the other. Your own symbols can not convey the meaning of the other. A new symbol is needed.

It follows then that you must necessarily create new symbols of the other. As with any act of creativity, discovery or revelation, interpretation is the result of a *dialectic*. It is as if you are in conversation with someone else. You must attempt to clearly understand what is being voiced by the other person. Listen carefully. But if there is to be a conversation, your own voice must also be part of and contribute to the dialogue. A conversation is the collaboration of both voices. In like fashion, meaning is to be rendered out of the dialogue between symbolizer, i.e., the interpreter, and phenomena to be symbolized, i.e., the other, though we would hope the voice of the other to be significantly louder. A *synthesis*, nevertheless, takes place. As you approach the story texts, listen to the voice of the other, it must predominate; but also acknowledge your own voice, and then let yourself imagine anew. Reflect on all these varied voices, symbols, images and meanings; re-arrange them in your head, and let them fall together in unforeseen ways.

And then apply your synthesis. Does it meet the criteria of *heuristic* validity, i.e., a more appropriate methodology of learning about the other, an increase in an overall understanding and appreciation of the other, and a humanizing of your relation with the other? If not, try again. Eye juggling involves the coordinated juggling of the eyes of the other and the self, and of eyes that have not yet seen, but that are about to.

Eye juggling is a *social activity*. This workbook is best approached in the context of collaborative group interactions. Find a partner. Form a discussion group. By so doing, not only can the story texts be heard read aloud, but each within the group can benefit from the ensuing spontaneous discussion and shared insights about the story texts. The eye of another may see what had been elusive to one's own.

To further assist you in your interpretation of a story text, a series of *discussion questions* are offered. The questions attempt to spawn additional reflection on the story texts by presenting perspectives and issues not readily apparent. It is as if you are in dialogue with another who is also eye juggling the same text. The questions are not to be answered as if for an "exam," with an expectation of eliciting comprehensive and "correct" responses. You simply do not have enough text materials presented to you in this workbook to even attempt such. And, more importantly, there can be no "correct" answers, only your heuristic interpretations. The questions are intended to probe and stimulate your reflections.

As you undertake each story text, you are encouraged to refer to the appropriate discussion questions listed toward the back of this workbook. Using the interpretative method just outlined, venture responses to the questions. Write out your responses in a journal. The writing process can assist you in sorting out and clarifying your thoughts. Then, utilizing your own interpretations of the story texts along with your responses to the questions, make a comparison with the interpretations offered by others within your collaborative group. Agreement may not result. *Differing* and *alternative* interpretations of the story texts, in fact, are encouraged. Through a dialogue of differing points of view, through the juggling of a multitude of eyes, new interpretations can emerge. In order to better see through the eyes of others as well as to see clearly through your own, a myriad of eyes, all of various shapes, sizes and colors, need to be juggled.

A final consideration. While each of the story texts of this workbook can be approached in isolation from the others, taken together they do provide a historical and cultural context and framework within which any given text can be better understood. This is particularly evident in the first two texts, "Dream Animal" and "Feathers." They present information critical to many of the interpretations and the implications to be garnered from the subsequent story texts. It is suggested that before interpreting any one story text you first do an initial "once-over" of all the story texts. As you do so, don't get bogged down in the detail or an unfamiliar term or concept. Try gaining a sense of the "*big picture.*" It's easier to identify the trees if you know which forest you're in.

Stories: The Texts

Dream Animal[1]

In the University lab, you're closely examining the crystallized bone fragments and chipped stone. Each is considered in its archaeological context. The dating methods are applied with care--potassium argon, obsidian hydration, radiocarbon dating. You've studied primate ethology and human ethnology, and comparisons are made. From the bone and the stone, an archaeological record of human evolution is proposed.

* * * * *

In the beginning there was a void and darkness, without form or life. Some 10 billion years ago, the primeval hydrogen gases supercondensed and exploded; the "Big Bang" had occurred. The expanding hydrogen cloud whirled about at enormous velocity and with the sudden cooling, the flying atomic particles condensed and formed the galaxies, stars and planets. On one minute object in one of those billions of solar systems something unique was to occur. Life would come forth in a very special way.

* * * * *

On a planet we call Earth, between 18 and 11 million years ago, a dog-sized, 30 pound primate inhabited the great forests of India and Africa. Traveling from tree limb to tree limb and using

---

[1]For additional background, see Barfield 1957, Coomaraswamy 1934, Eliade 1954, Eiseley 1957, Fagan 1989, Kroeber 1952, 1963, Levi-Strauss 1966, Nasr 1968, Smith 1976 and White 1940.

all four of its own limbs to do so, *Ramapithecus* (*Rama*, a Hindu God, and *pithecus*, Greek for apes) subsisted on the fruit it foraged from its forest habitat. Not particularly well-adapted to its niche, *Ramapithecus* was slow-moving, produced few offspring and with its small teeth and claws, was not well endowed to protect itself. It existed in the safety the trees offered, a forest of trees in an ever-changing physical environment.

Living in a tree environment had fostered among the early primates two important adaptations--the opposable thumb and stereoscopic vision. The success in swinging from branch to branch was dependent on an ability to accurately judge the distance between branches and then to be able to firmly grab hold of a branch. Hand dexterity, eye-hand coordination, and enhanced visual perception became critical attributes of the primate.

The world for *Ramapithecus* and other early primates was a world of praxis, of plant and animal living in interaction with the physical environment. This quadruped lived in the immediacy of its own actions and reactions to the physical events around it. Instinct, driven by natural selection, and conditioning, driven by interaction with the environment, formed the basis of its cerebral-based judgements.

This is not to suggest that a world of thought and spirit did not also exist 18 million years ago. It is that *Ramapithecus* had *no comprehension* of the existence of such a world. *Ramapithecus* had little capacity to create and use symbols. Without symbols, there can be no conceptualization. *Ramapithecus* had no knowledge of "self," no self awareness. It had no knowledge of "other," as a self separate from "other" creatures. It had no knowledge of "time," of its own history, destiny and mortality. *Ramapithecus* was very much a part of the natural world in which it found itself.

By 3 million years ago, the African forests had given way to grassland savanna. The ancestral inheritors of *Ramapithecus* found themselves in a changed environmental niche that necessitated a change in themselves if they were to survive. An adaptation of swinging through the trees no longer served the primates now roaming amongst the tall grasses. For some of those primates a unique form of adaptation was about to emerge. Those primates were known as *Australopithecus* (Latin for "South African ape") and the larger brained *Homo habilis* (Latin for "handy man").

As a consequence of the shrinking forests, there were less food stuffs available, and primates had to forage farther from home bases. Amongst the tall grasses, visibility was limited. The saber-toothed tiger could easily approach without warning. One form of adaptation was bipedal locomotion. On two legs as opposed to four, the primate could range farther afield, see better over the tall grasses, and, with freed hands, could carry food stuffs back to a camp. There was a selective advantage among those primates who could walk upright. The hominid had emerged.

Idle hands make for the devil's work. With freed hands, in combination with the enhanced hand dexterity and eye-hand coordination that had evolved while swinging among the trees, hands could now create tools. Attempting to butcher an animal was tough going with small teeth suited for chewing, not cutting. Crude as they were, the sharp edges of stone tools allowed access to a new food source, one rich in protein and one condensed into a small, portable package. Less time was spent foraging about for food and could now be spent in other pursuits. Meat, scavenged from the kill of another animal, would now supplement plant foods. While remaining predominantly a plant eater, the size of the meat-eating primates nevertheless increased. They now stood tall at four foot and weighed up to eighty pounds.

But to fashion a stone tool, the tool must first be imagined. As crude as the tool may have been, the conceptualization of it was not. A tremendous adaptive advantage existed for those primates with an increased brain capacity. It enabled them to envision an image of a tool within a stone, to bring forth that image through the coordination of their fingers and thus release the tool from the stone, and then to communicate this entire body of "how to" knowledge to their offspring. Cranium capacity increased in *Homo habilis* to 800 cubic centimeters (a modern chimpanzee is at 300 cc and *Homo sapiens* at 1500 cc). The world of symbolic meaning had been entered. Tools of all kinds, shelter, clothing and fire were now imagined into being. And with these images came rudimentary systems of self-expression and communication. Fire soon replaced fur, and symbols gradually replaced genes as this primate's primary form of adaptation to its environment.

The erect posture had morphological repercussions for the throat of the primate. Vocal cords, tongue and larynx were stimulated, and a greater range of sounds could now be produced vocally. Speech was possible. A much more precise form of communication resulted, and more information could be exchanged. The transmission and learning of symbols was greatly enhanced.

With erect bipedal locomotion, the pelvic structure of the primate became more massive, supporting the internal organs that now gravitated toward the lower stomach instead of from the spine. For the female pelvis, this meant that the birth canal became smaller. And together with the increased size of the cranium, young had to be born earlier, physically premature as a result. The young primate was not born autonomous, but was very dependent on others for physical survival and, most importantly, for the acquisition of an ever-expanding body of symbolic knowledge. A mother-child bonding grew. Mothers nurtured with breast and defended from beast, and taught with symbols the skills needed for survival. The seeds of social cooperation and the family were firmly planted.

In turn, with mothers spending more time with their young and less at food gathering, and with mothers less able to ward off the saber-toothed tigers with infants in arm, the mother-child bond was vulnerable. To the mother-child family was joined the male. He could help protect, and he could help secure food. The family unit was enlarged, and a male/female gender division of labor emerged. Male roles oscillated around the hunt for game animals and the protection from those animals that would hunt them, while female roles tended toward gathering plant foods and care of the young and the aged. The value of social cooperation was further enhanced.

With the tendency toward gender role specification also came a physical dimorphism. Among the males there was a marked increase in height and weight over females. Gross musculature became greater, hearts stronger and blood cells per unit volume of blood increased. More blood was lost in the hunt and in the defense from a hunt. This sexual dimorphism is unique, not exhibited by other primates.

Any view of the noble males coming to the rescue of the females and their offspring must be tempered by an understanding of the rewards of that association. Other changes were occurring in the hominid primate. There was a suppression of the estrus cycle, and females became continuously sexually active. No other primate is so oriented. The size, both in relative and absolute terms, of the male penis became larger than any other primate, including the gorilla. With the loss of body hair and the softening of skin of the female, sexual tactility became important, again unique among primates. These are virtually the only primates to engage in face-to-face sexual intercourse. The male-female bond was strengthened because of the gratification each received from the other.

Taken altogether, the economic and survival values along with the sexual pleasures set the stage for the development of the most elaborate expression of sexual union among any animal, i.e., human courting and marriage rituals and kinship rules. For the individual of the species, there was thus an increasing sense of incompleteness and a need for the companionship only another could provide.

In addition to the cooperative male-female bonding, a significant adaptive consequence of the increased sexual activity was an increased frequency of births. The population grew. And as mothers now tended to have several infants to care for simultaneously, the association of a mother-child-father into a cooperative family unit was further enhanced.

* * * * *

For a rather timid primate, survival in the physical world depended upon being removed from that world and on creating a world of its own fabrication, an artificial environment that would mediate the forces of the natural world. It was a wondrous garment of symbolic meanings that clothed this primate, bringing forth the world of culture, of story and of values. Symbols replaced genes, and fire replaced fur. Beginning with *Australopithecus* and *Homo habilis*, there emerged what Loren Eiseley has called the *Dream Animal*.[2]

If symbols are seen as the fiber and thread, then *culture* is the fabric that clothes the Dream Animal. The cultural world of the Dream Animal, the only animal to have created an all-pervasive conceptual world, entails social, ideological, psychological and ecological domains.

The social is the domain of technology, economics, politics, family, and aesthetic and religious organizations--the organizing of people's activities. Cooperation rather than competition or aggression characterized the original tone of this domain.

The ideological is the cultural domain of awareness of and involvement in thought and spirit, in imagination and dreams. An animal became aware of its own soul and of its own mortality for the first time. This is the domain of the aesthetic, philosophical and spiritual search for meaning, identity, origins and destiny, for beauty, for love, for truth. Interestingly, the Dream Animal is the only animal who can tell a non-truth, who can lie. To lie is not just to deceive. Other animals can do that; a nesting prairie chicken darts as a decoy for its young when a coyote approaches. To lie is to conceptually and consciously choose to convey a non-truth to someone else. Despite the preponderance of cooperation and compassion shown toward its

---

[2]See Eiseley 1957.

own kind, the Dream Animal is also the only species that can hate, have prejudice and kill its own kind in systematic ways, i.e., has wars.

Within the psychological domain are processes of communication and enculturation that contribute to the formation of concepts of self and other. The psychological is the domain from which roles are defined, self-esteem built and motivations directed.

The ecological domain of culture includes the various modes of societal adaptation to the environment, e.g., gatherer-hunter, horticultural, agricultural, industrial; modes that have allowed the Dream Animal to inhabit virtually every environmental niche on this planet. It is the only animal capable of doing so. Out of the ecological domain has emerged the knowledge of technologies and sciences.

If culture provides the fabric that clothes the Dream Animal, then *story* provides the design for that fabric and the particular weave for those fibers. Fiber is woven into a whole garment. The words and images of story embody the collective wisdom and understandings of a particular people, in a particular landscape, in a particular interaction with their world. Story embodies the collectivity of a people and a place, enshrining the imprint of rock and spirit, of technology and animal, of knowing and feeling, of humans and Gods.

But story is much more than just the integration of the various cultural domains, though it is that. Story is also the themes and motifs involving heroes and tricksters, the quests and transformations that vitalize the Dream Animal with a character and quality, with an ethos. Story is the plot of the human narrative told through the words of cultural expressions. Story is culture personified; the Dream Animal is imbued with persona.

Embedded within and throughout the cultural story of the Dream Animal are values. If symbols are the fibers, and culture the fabric, and story the weave and design, then *values* are the elasticity of the Dream Animal's garment. Values provide the flexibility and resilience, the emotional tone and moral disposition to the fiber and design. The cultural story is infused with spark and momentum, the Dream Animal with drive. Values provide emotionally-charged, moral concepts that assist the Dream Animal in making judgements and preparing for action. The garment and the Dream Animal are brought to life.

Thus, as with the individual of the species, so the species itself had a sense of incompleteness and a need for companionship. It is the companionship that only the "cultural story" would provide. In the telling of its story, the Dream Animal has come into being. Without *culture*, without *story*, without *values* there can be no Dream Animal.

Because of the emergence of this remarkable garment, this should not imply that the Dream Animal is the only animal capable of symbolizing. Other animals certainly can. Dolphins and chimpanzees, for instance, have a rudimentary ability to use symbols. Dolphins communicate symbolically. For the chimpanzee in its natural setting, to strip the bark from a twig and thrust the sticky twig into a termite hill, only to retrieve a food source high in protein, presupposes a symbolic ability to conceptualize the entire process prior to bringing forth the tool. What then distinguishes the Dream Animal from other animals is the degree to which the former symbolizes. Instincts derived by natural selection and behavioral conditioning resulting from interactions with the environment predominate the cerebral-based judgements of other animals, and not an ability to symbolize and fabricate an entire world of culture and story. The world of the animal is a world of signs. The world of the Dream Animal is a world of symbols, of culture, and of story.

* * * * *

Despite societal variation, some form of rite of passage is at the core and foundation of virtually every Dream Animal educational, social and spiritual dynamic. Whether it be in an individual vision quest or the collective Crow Sun Dance, in the initiation rituals associated with the Aranda Karora totemic society or with becoming an Iglulik shaman or Crow *akbaalia*, or even in the oral narrative of Burnt Face, the symbolic structures and processes of each expression encompasses a rite of passage. In tribal-oriented societies, the entire life-cycle of an individual, from childhood to old age, for both men and women, is marked by a series of rites of passage.

In Euro-American society, while much less overt and pervasive, rites of passage are nevertheless operative and critical. Induction into the military or a fraternal organization, or participation in a religious retreat: all entail rites of passage. To a certain extent, the educational system, from kindergarten to high school and college is a rite of passage.

Rites of passage serve not only to publicly acknowledge the transition from one educational, social or spiritual status to another, but more fundamentally, to facilitate and bring about such a transformation in the first place.[3] Four universal components to the symbolic structuring of any rite of passage are evident. These structural components can be found expressed not only in ritual behavior, such as initiation ceremonies, but also in the literary motifs of oral and written literature. In the instance of American Indian oral narratives, next in prevalence to the trickster motif, is the orphan quest motif. The structural components of a rite of passage can be readily identified in the orphan quest motif in this oral literature. Let me outline here what are extremely elaborate and complex processes. While my reference point is tribal-oriented societies, rites of passage pervade the entirety of the human experience.

First, a rite of passage presupposes an orphaned status. The individual neophyte is symbolically understood as an *"orphan,"* somehow incomplete. In oral literature themes, the individual is represented as alone and often abused and bullied by an adversary, in need of help. Whether it be in ritual or literature, the individual is as an impoverished child, either without parents or lacking in some significant attribute, such as the knowledge and skills of an adult, the integration provided by social kinship

---

[3]For additional discussion on rites of passage, see Eliade 1964, Turner 1967 and van Gennep 1906.

or the spiritual insight and power of a shaman. Something vital is missing. A void needs to be filled.

Second, a rite of passage involves a *separation, a journey* and *a sacrifice*. The neophyte may be physically removed by the elders from his or her village and taken to a "bush school" for a period lasting several weeks or even months. The neophyte himself may venture on a vision quest to a far mountain site, the quest lasting up to several days. An apprenticeship may occur, initiated by the neophyte with an established sage, teacher or healer and lasting for many years. It could also be the case that an individual, often while ill and close to death, is involuntarily visited by a spirit guardian. In all these instances, a symbolic "journey," full of challenges of all kinds, transpires. It is a journey to a world distinct from the ordinary. "All true wisdom is to be found far from the dwellings of men."

The neophyte enters a "liminal state," "betwixt and between," removed from the mundane and the ordinary. The neophyte is physically and socially cut off from the only world he or she has known. In the "bush school," the neophyte goes nameless and unwashed, without social definition and status. In the instance of a vision quest, the neophyte will undergo several purification procedures--a sweat bath, rubbing self with sweet sage and incensing of sweet cedar, for instance. The site of the vision quest may be a distant butte or hill, far away from the human community. At the site, a bed of sage will be prepared. The individual humbles himself, showing total humility. While at the site, which may last from two to five days, a sacrifice is given, going without food and water. You "die" a little as you watch your life leave your body under the hot sun. As the Inuit say, when you go out and seek a vision, you must have an "intimacy with death."

Any rite of passage involves a "ritual death." To "die" is to sacrifice and give up something. If a quest is to be successful, if one is to receive a vision, the neophyte must offer up what is most cherished. Reciprocity and a gift exchange between the self and the spirit world must occur. The neophyte offers up his or her food and water, perhaps his own flesh as small pieces are cut from the arm, and most importantly, his or her own sincerity. During the "bush school," the sacrifice may be expressed as a circumcision, subincision, tooth-knocking out or some other form of scarification ritual. The circumcision and subincision "cutting" vividly symbolizes not only an offering up of flesh but a severing from one gender identity and an affiliating with another, i.e., the boys have been taken from their mothers' arms and brought into the world of men. In all instances, the offering of oneself assumes two active agents: a giver and a receiver.

To "die" is also to be brought to the threshold of the sacred, to be torn from the living, separated and stripped from one's mundane existence and identity. Without a name and social conventions, the neophyte is rendered void, as nothing, emptied, and thus very receptive. Stripping away the mundane reveals and exposes within oneself what is most essential to the neophyte, the soul. During the initiation, "you watch as your flesh is ripped from your body and you see your own bones, you get down to your bones."

Third, a rite of passage involves the *acquisition of power* and *knowledge*. Having been rendered receptive, as warmed wax, the neophyte can be molded in the imprint of the sacred. The soul is exposed to the spiritual teachings and sacred archetypes. It is during the "liminal state" that the neophyte may witness the creation time as the mythic beings are brought forth in the performance of the great ceremonials and in the telling of the rich body of mythology. In the "bush school," the initiated elders dance and tell of the sacred truths during the night and disseminate the social and economic knowledge required of an adult during the day. The wisdom and knowledge of the ancestors can be gained as the great mysteries are revealed.

While on a lonely butte, a vision and adoption by a spirit guardian can occur. If the gift of oneself is judged worthy and accepted, a vision is rendered. The previous state of two active agents is transcended, becoming as one, in union, with ordinary time and space dissolved. The neophyte communicates with and learns of the spiritual truths. He or she is instructed and guided by an animal spirit as it appears in the vision. Rules of respect and taboos to honor the spirit guardian are revealed. The vision establishes an adoption relation, a parent-child dyad, as the neophyte is adopted by a spirit guardian. The Buffalo or Eagle is now as a father, a parent to the neophyte. The adoption solidifies a spiritual kinship, a father who is close by to guide throughout one's life.

Fourth, any rite of passage involves *affirmation* and *rebirth*. With the knowledge of the ancestors gained or the vision of a spiritual guardian received, the individual returns to the ordinary world, his or her self redefined, with a new status. He or she returns triumphant, overcoming what had been an "orphaned status." The linkage with this new status and knowledge may be overtly symbolized and maintained through the possession of a medicine bundle and medicine songs. Having come down from the mountain top or out of the bush, the wisdom and knowledge of the ancestors is applied, wounds are healed, and the power to fly or cure is affected.

In passing through a rite of passage, the various educational, social and spiritual transitions through which an individual moves are thus not only publicly acknowledged, but the transitions themselves are accomplished. The ascendancy to a new status is socially validated. A child becomes an adult, redefined in the eyes of others. The individual is also offered a means to shed one identity and orientation for another, thus acquiring and re-orienting his or her entire world view, socially, economically and spiritually. New knowledge and skills, new responsibilities and obligations, new awarenesses and sensitivities are effectively imparted and assimilated. Rites of passage transform the very being of an individual, providing a mechanism for life-cycle transitions.

* * * * *

What is the physical health and well-being of those who carve for Sedna and dance to Karora, those who painted images in Les Trois Freres and tell of Burnt Face? What is the quality of life in gatherer-hunter society, for those living in ancient times as well as the more recent? The social philosopher Thomas Hobbes in his *Leviathan* (1651) had characterized it as a life with "no knowledge of the face of the earth; no account of time; no arts; no letters; no society; and which is worst of all, continual fear, and danger of violent death; and the life of man, solitary, poor, nasty, brutish, and short."

Archaeological and ethnographic studies over the last thirty years have re-written our images of the gatherer-hunter Dream Animal of the past and the contemporary, and have helped dispel many commonly held stereotypes. Certainly variations occur and exceptions abound, but a coherent imagery is emerging. What, indeed, is the quality of life in gatherer-hunter society?

Let me offer a brief comparison of the differing levels of resources needed to sustain gatherer-hunter and Euro-American societies.[4] The comparison will focus on the daily consumption of energy per capita in each of six types of societies and will be measured in terms of equivalent kilocalories.

In paleolithic society, the primary source of energy is derived from the food stuffs that are individually consumed and is the equivalent to approximately **2,000** kilocalories needed per day per capita.

In historic and contemporary gatherer-hunter society, energy is derived from food consumed and from firewood used for heating and cooking. The equivalent of **5,000** kilocalories are needed daily per capita (2,000 kilo. food energy and 3,000 kilo. firewood energy).

In horticultural society, domesticated plants harvested by hand from gardens supplanted the gathering of wild plants. Domesticated animals also contribute to the energy source. The equivalent of **12,000** kilocalories are required (4,000 kilo. food, 4,000 kilo. firewood and 4,000 kilo. domesticated animals).

In agricultural society, the plow, draft animal and field replace the garden. Coal is often used as a fuel source along

---

[4]See Cook 1971.

with wind and/or water. Transportation is aided by animals. The equivalent of **26,000** kilocalories are needed daily (7,000 kilo. food, 6,000 kilo. firewood, 12,000 kilo. domesticated animal and 1,000 kilo. coal).

In industrial society, the steam and gas engine are the backbone of energy production and consumption. The equivalent of **77,000** kilocalories are required per capita per day (24,000 kilo. food, 7,000 kilo. firewood, 32,000 kilo. domesticated animals, and 14,000 kilo. coal).

In technological society, electricity via coal, water and nuclear energy resources is the cornerstone of energy production and consumption. The equivalent of from **230,000** to **273,000** kilocalories are needed per individual each day (91,000 kilo. food, 10,000 kilo. firewood, 33,000 kilo. domesticated animals, 63,000 kilo. coal and 33,000 kilo. electricity).

Our Euro-American society is comprised of elements of both the industrial and technological societal orientations. The comparison of a contemporary gatherer-hunter **5,000** kilocalorie consumption level with an industrial-technological **77,000-273,000** kilocalorie consumption level offers a most remarkable contrast.

It is often perceived that with the advent of technological society there has been a significant reduction in the number of hours of human labor needed for production and an increase in leisure time. This perception is not the case. The amount of work output directed at food gathering, preparation and related subsistence activities in gatherer-hunter society is typically the equivalent of **20-25** hours per week. Much more time is engaged in ritual, social and recreational activities. There is, in fact, far greater leisure time in gatherer-hunter societies than there is in our own industrial society. In technological society, a 40-hour work week has become necessary for minimal subsistence. Three weeks of vacation plus holidays is a norm. With all the labor-saving appliances, the urban American homemaker puts in an average of 55 hours per week in household-related activities. In the 1920s, without the benefits of these devices, an average of 52 hours of housework was expended. Even the medieval serf of Europe had 115 days off for festivals.

The quality of gatherer-hunter diet is also most revealing.[5] With societal exceptions such as the Eskimo, wild plant foods typically account for 60-70% of the diet. Because of the gender role dichotomy of "man the hunter" and "woman the gatherer," women actually contributed more food stuffs to the family than did their counterparts, though often without receiving the glory and recognition. This ratio of a 30-40% meat contribution thus existed throughout a million-year history of humanity. The ratio was only altered with the domestication of plants and reliance on various crop foods. Meat consumption was thereafter significantly reduced. Then came the modern American diet, with the introduction of a newly constituted meat form, rich in fats.

For the historic and contemporary gatherer-hunter, typically **2,150** calories are consumed daily. In the paleolithic diet, an estimated **3,000** calories were consumed on a daily basis. These levels of calorie consumption are comparable with the United States Department of Agriculture recommended minimum of 1,975 calories.

In gatherer-hunter society protein amounts around **90** grams per day are achieved while the paleolithic diet was at **250** grams. These levels are comparable or exceed the actual U.S. average consumption which ranges from 50-125 grams. Of interest, early *Homo sapiens* and *Neanderthals* of 75,000 years ago averaged 6 inches taller than agricultural peoples of 8,000 years ago, and remained so up to a 100 years ago. Today, we are now as tall as we once were.

Paleolithic fat consumption was at **71** grams per day (30 g. animal and 41 g. plant), representing 21% of the total daily dietary energy source. The U.S. average consumption represents

---

[5]See Eaton and Konner 1985 for a discussion on paleolithic diet, and Lee 1968 and Sahlins 1972 for a discussion of historic and contemporary gatherer-hunter diet.

42% of the diet, with 30% a U.S.D.A. recommended.   A
significant portion of the U.S. fat consumption is of saturated
fats.

Sodium levels in the paleolithic diet were at **690** milligrams,
compared with the U.S. average consumption of 2,300-6,900
mg. per day.

Calcium intake levels in the paleolithic were at **1,580**
milligrams, compared with an average 740 mg. per day in the
U.S.   Of note, this calcium level was reached without dairy
products, e.g., cheese or milk, but was a result of the way animal
foods are prepared and consumed, i.e., inclusion of animal bone.

Remarkably, ascorbic acid was at **392** milligrams per day,
compared with an average U.S. consumption of 88 mg.

Paleolithic fiber intake was at **46** grams per day, compared
with an average U.S. of 20 grams.

As with the quality of the diet, the quality of historic and
contemporary gatherer-hunter health is rather revealing.
Typically, there are fewer diseases compared with industrial
society.   Prior to European contact, there was no diabetes, no
stroke or heart disease, most varieties of cancer were absent, no
hypertension or senility.   There was also an absence of many of
the infectious diseases characteristic of industrial society.   There
were higher infant mortality rates, however.   But if infancy was
survived, over 10% of the population lived over 60 years, which
is comparable to many industrial societies.

Given the social equality and the kinship sharing
characteristic of gatherer-hunter society, hunger is not
"institutionalized."   Gatherer-hunter society is typically an
equalitarian society.   No group and seldom an individual goes
without, unless a local disaster causes all to go without. Poverty,
a creation of class distinction and an unequal distribution of
resources, is to be found in agricultural and industrial societies.

Keep in mind that the gatherer-hunter orientation has
represented over ninety-nine percent of all of Dream Animal
history.   Plant and animal domestication and our technologically-
oriented society is a relatively new experiment in the human

experience. Also keep in mind that the quality of diet and health found among gatherer-hunter peoples is achieved with relatively minimal resource demands and a "simple" technology. It is a technology that provides an efficient means of utilizing the available resources.

An argument can be made, as Marshal Sahlins has made, that there is affluence in gatherer-hunter society, the "original affluent society."[6] I would suggest that the affluence is, in fact, greater than that found in industrial society. Such is the case if affluence is a measure of the ratio of the means and products available, i.e., the technological knowledge and goods produced, relative to the desired wants, i.e., the expectations. We are, of course, speaking of the material affluence relating to food, health and physical comfort. In gatherer-hunter society, we find that the material expectations of the people closely match their means to obtain those expectations. What people desire is obtained. It is acknowledged that what is desired in gatherer-hunter society may not be even remotely similar to that desired in industrial society. Nevertheless, in gatherer-hunter society, the desires of food, health and physical comfort are fundamentally secured. What is not as easily obtainable are desires relating to social, aesthetic and spiritual fulfillments. Here the quests continue. In contrast, the quest for material affluence has become a driving force in industrial society; while the quests for social, aesthetic and spiritual fulfillments continue but are apparently less overtly emphasized. All things considered, given the quality of diet and of health, and the relative affluence, life in gatherer-hunter society is anything but "nasty, brutish and short."[7]

---

[6]See Sahlins 1972.

[7]These comments are not presented to suggest a call for a "return to the primitive." We must avoid romanticizing the gatherer-hunter as our "noble savage." After all, the gatherer-hunter seldom has had an opportunity to "tax" the "carrying capacity" of their lands. Their "simple" technology more than met their physical needs and

* * * * *

You've just entered one of the caves, leaving behind the sun's light and today's date.[8] It's a long passage, with many side passages leading off in other directions. You descend deep into the earth, among the damp and the stalactites. The only sound is of water dripping from the ceilings and of your breathing. The only light is that which you carry. At places you must creep along low on all fours. You lose your sense of time and place, no longer sure how long you've been in the cave or in what direction you're moving. These are caverns which have never served as places of human shelter, habitat, or home. But then, as now, these are places visited only on special occasions, for special purposes; though those who came before, undoubtedly came for very different purposes.

You've emerged into the great gallery. Before you are the images of hundreds of animal drawings, many overlapping each other, animals such as wild horses, bison, ibex and reindeer. They are images rich in earthen colors: yellows, reds, browns, and black. Many are life-sized, and all are rather realistically portrayed. Some of the images are painted over natural bulges in the rock, giving the animals a further sense of relief and life. There are, however, few representations of human images, and those you find are simple, stick-like images.

You've journeyed to Europe and are now viewing the cave paintings of the Upper Paleolithic period, dating to 18,000 years ago. Three of the over seventy cave sites of northern Spain and France are visited: Altamira, Lascaux and Les Trois Freres. As you gaze among the varied images, four catch your eyes.

---

expectations. By comparison, the vastly expanded population of our contemporary world necessitates a resource base and technological infrastructure of a magnitude incomprehensible to the gatherer-hunter.

[8]For additional enthnographic background, see Campbell 1959 and Fagan 1989.

The first image is from Altamira, in northern Spain. The bison is painted in vivid reds and black.

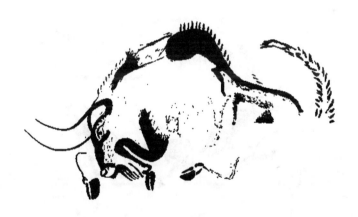

Your second image comes from Lascaux cave in central France. A great bison was speared, apparently by the crudely drawn human figure. As mentioned, human images are few. This particular one is interesting because of its bird-like features, i.e., bird's head and bird's hands, and staff with perched bird attached atop. Images of birds are even rarer than those few of humans. Also notice what appears to be a phallus on the human figure.

The third image comes from the walls of the Les Trois Freres cave in the French Pyrenees. Amongst a vast assemblage of overlapping animal images (not presented here) we see a human-like figure with a bow in hand (apparently a hunting or musical bow) and in pursuit of two unidentified animals.

In the innermost region of the Les Trois Freres cave we come across a most astonishing image. It is painted in black and stands two-and-a-half feet tall. The figure has the body of a human, the horns and ears of a reindeer, the tail and location of the penis of a horse, the hands that resemble the paws of a feline, and the face of a lion or perhaps an owl?

* * * * *

Through the stone, an image of yourself is glimpsed. And the chipped stone and crystallized bone are placed with care back on the shelf behind the glass and the lock.

Feathers[9]

The *Ashkisshe*, "imitation lodge," the Sun Dance is into its third day. Most of the hundred and twenty dancers, men and women, are up dancing strong, "charging" the center pole. Two days before, in the prayers of those who were about to use the chain saw, assistance was sought of the Cottonwood Tree, green with foliage. Permission was asked, and permission was given. The tree was cut down and moved with care to the field that would hold the Sun Dance.

The cottonwood center pole now stands watching over the dancers. Below its two forks, the eagle is hung to the east and the buffalo head faces west. From the lips of the dancers, eagle-bone whistles sound the cry of the bird, and from the lodge entrance, drumbeat and voice offer song. Each of the dancers has made a prayer to *Akbaatatdia*, the Maker of All Things First, a vow to give of him or herself so that another might be helped. All have gone without food and water; all now dance under the hundred degree heat of the July sun. From within the circular lodge of freshly cut lodgepoles and cottonwood brush, open to the sky, the center pole is "charged" again.

Deaxkaashe, Eagle, circles high above, watching over all those who sound his cry.

You begin to sway, no longer able to "charge" and dance back from the center pole in a straight line. You continue for some time, though no longer in time. And then you take a "hard fall," collapsing to the ground. Others jump to their feet and

---

[9]For additional background, see Bohr 1934 and 1958, Heisenberg 1958, Frey 1987, Wheeler 1973 and Zukav 1979.

without disturbing you, cover your body with cattails and sage cuttings. The dance continues, though with one less dancer.

* * * * *

"He's dreaming now," said Tweedledee, "and what do you think he's dreaming about?"

Alice said, "Nobody can guess that."

"Why, about you!" Tweedledee exclaimed, clapping his hands triumphantly. "And if he left off dreaming about you, where do you suppose you'd be?"

"Where I am now, of course," said Alice.

"Not you!" Tweedledee retorted contemptuously. "You'd be nowhere. Why you're only a sort of thing in his dream!"

"If that there King was to wake," added Tweedledum, "you'd go out--bang!--just like a candle!"

"I shouldn't!" Alice exclaimed indignantly. "Besides, if I'm only a sort of thing in his dream, what are you, I should like to know?"

"Ditto." said Tweedledum.

"Ditto, ditto!" cried Tweedledee.

He shouted this so loud that Alice couldn't help saying, "Hush! You'll be waking him, I'm afraid, if you make so much noise."

And so Lewis Carroll wrote in *Through the Looking Glass* (1871).

* * * * *

"We are what we imagine. Our very existence consists in our imagination of ourselves. Our best destiny is to imagine, at least, completely, who and what, and that we are. The greatest tragedy that can befall us is to go unimagined."

So wrote the Kiowa poet N. Scott Momaday (1934-present) in "Man Made of Words."

* * * * *

For Samuel Taylor Coleridge (1772-1834), the English poet and author of "The Ancient Mariner" and "Kubla Khan," imagination is essential for humanity. Imagination is the act of knowing and of feeling the life within all of the world, and of participating in that life.

* * * * *

When can a single event generate opposite impressions by the same observer at the same time? This was the question originally posed by the British philosopher, George Berkeley (1685-1753) in *Three Dialogues between Hylas and Philonous* (1713). Take three basins of water: one hot, one cold, and the third lukewarm. Now place one hand in the hot water, while the other is placed in the cold, and leave them in the water for several minutes. Then plunge both hands into the lukewarm water. Does not the cold hand sense warm water, while the hot hand sense in the very same basin cold water? The world is never as it seems, as something absolute and given. For what appears to us as the world is always influenced by our interactions with it, by what we bring into the experience.

For Berkeley, the world can not be directly known by what is experienced through our senses. But rather, what is knowable in the world is what is first conceived of in the mind. The world is, in fact, what is conceived--*esse est percipi*, "to be is to be perceived." A phenomenon has being and existence to the extent that its properties are a conceived idea, be it a "tree" or a "wilderness."

* * * * *

"Knowledge comes about in so far as the object known is within the knower."

So wrote Saint Thomas Aquinas (1225-1274) in *Summa Theologica*.

* * * * *

"Every person is a special kind of artist." Meister Eckhart (1260-1327), a German Dominican theologian, was convinced of it; and Ananda Coomaraswamy, the eminent scholar of Buddhist and Hindu philosophy, echoed the same sentiment in his book, *The Transformation of Nature in Art* (1934).

* * * * *

Sticks and stones can break my bones, but names can surely kill me.

* * * * *

The medicine bundle is opened, its sacred objects lie upon the elk hide--an eagle-feather fan, leather effigy of an elk and braid of sweet grass. With the tobacco of cigarettes, prayers are offered. The parents bring their infant forward and place it in the arms of the child's clan uncle. A name had come in a dream and is now being bestowed on the child. If the name agrees with the child, the child will become the words of the name. The name will protect; it will guide. And it will be cherished. Should the name not agree with the child, the child will soon become sickly, and a new name will be sought.

The Crow people have an expression, *dasshussua*, meaning "breaking with the mouth." That which comes through the mouth, words, has the power to affect the world. In the same manner that an "Indian" name protects, a spoken pledge is to be fulfilled or accidents seem to happen; one never says goodbye, for it is too final; and one never speaks of an illness, for it may come about. And not only words, but the symbolic images of art, of ritual dance and costume, and of architecture not only describe and define phenomenon but help bring about that which they describe. All words, all symbols are animated with a power to effect the world.

* * * * *

Locust is the first to come up the "reed of emergence" into this, the Fifth World, the earth surface world, followed by First Man and First Woman, Pollen Boy, Lightning God and Talking God, and all the other *Diyin Dinee*, the Holy People.[10] All around is water and darkness. There are no peoples, but there are many monsters. There is much *hocho*--disorder and ugliness.

At the Emergence Place, the Holy People decide to build a sweathouse, like a hogan though much larger. First Man brings his medicine bundle with him into the sweat bath, the bundle

---

[10]The story text is a segment from the Navajo Emergence story. For additional ethnographic background, see Mitchell 1978, Witherspoon 1977 and Wyman 1970.

containing four jewels--turquoise, white shell, abalone and
obsidian. In the heat and the steam, the Holy People whisper to
each other and, with the knowledge of *hozho*--beauty and
harmony, plan the earth-surface world. They think of the *biiasti*,
the "in-standing ones," the inner forms of all things. Then the
Holy People speak the words of the world and sing the world
into being.

> The earth will be,
>> the mountains will be...,
> The earth will be,
>> from ancient times with me there is knowledge
>> of it.
> The mountains will be,
>> from ancient times with me there is knowledge
>> of it....
> The earth will be,
>> from the very beginning I have thought it.
> The mountains will be,
>> from the very beginning I have thought it....
> The earth will be,
>> from the ancient times I speak it.
> The mountains will be,
>> from the ancient times I speak it....
> The earth will be,
>> the mountains will be,...
>>> and so it will be. (from the Beginning
>>> of the World Song)

And the rivers and mountains, the sun and moon, come forth;
each with *biiasti*. And there is *Saah Naaghaii Bikeh Hozho*,
"continual reoccurring long life in an environment of beauty and
harmony."

> Earth's feet have become my feet
>> by means of these I shall live on.
> Earth's legs have become my legs
>> by means of these I shall live on.

Earth's body has become my body
      by means of this I shall live on.
Earth's mind has become my mind
      by means of this I shall live on.
Earth's voice has become my voice
      by means of this I shall live on.
Earth's headplume has become my headplume
      by means of this I shall live on.

The cord-like extension from the top of its head
      is cord-like from the top of my head as by
      means of this I shall live on.
There are mountains encircling it and
      Hozho extends up their slopes,
          by means of these it will be hozho as I
          shall live on.

Saah Naaghaii Bikeh Hozho I shall be,
Before me it will be hozho as I live on,
Behind me it will be hozho as I live on,
Below me it will be hozho as I live on,
Above me it will be hozho as I live on.

Hozho has been restored.
Hozho has been restored.
Hozho has been restored.
Hozho has been restored. (from the Blessingway Song)

And there is also *hocho*. Monsters persist--Hunger, Poverty, Lice Man, Laziness.

In the heat and steam, the Holy People think the world and then speak the world into being.

* * * * *

In the beginning of creation, when God made heaven and earth, the earth was without form and void, with darkness over the face of the abyss, and a mighty wind that swept over the

surface of the waters. God said, "Let there be light;" and there
was light; and God saw that the light was good, and he separated
the light from darkness. He called the light day, and the
darkness night. So evening came, and morning came, the first
day.

God said, "Let there be a vault between the waters, to
separate water from water." So God made the vault, and
separated the water under the vault from the water above it, and
it was so; and God called the vault heaven. Evening came, and
morning came, a second day.

God said, "Let the waters under the heavens be gathered into
one place, so that the dry land may appear;" and so it was. God
called the dry land earth, and the gathered waters he called seas;
and God saw that it was good.

Then God said, "Let the earth produce fresh growth, let there
be on the earth plants bearing seed, fruit-trees bearing fruit each
with seed according to its kind." So it was; the earth yielded
fresh growth, plants bearing seed according to their kind and
trees bearing fruit each with seeds according to its kind; and God
saw that it was good. Evening came, and morning came, a third
day....

God said, "Let the earth bring forth living creatures,
according to their kind: cattle, reptiles, and wild animals, all
according to their kind." So it was; God made the wild animals,
cattle, and all reptiles, each according to its kind; and he saw that
it was good. (Genesis 1:1-13, 24-25)

* * * * *

So God formed out of the ground all the wild animals and all
the birds of the heaven. He brought them to man to see what he
would call them, and whatever the man called each living
creature, that was its name. Thus the man gave names to all
cattle, to the birds of the heaven, and to every wild animal; but
for the man himself no partner had yet been found. And so the
Lord God put the man into a trance, and while he slept, he took
one of his ribs and closed the flesh over the place. The Lord
God then built up the rib, which he had taken out of the man,

into a woman. He brought her to the man, and the man said: "Now this, at last--bone from my bones, flesh from my flesh!-- this shall be called woman, for from man was this taken." That is why a man leaves his father and his mother and is united to his wife, and the two become one flesh. Now they were both naked, the man and his wife, but they had no feelings of shame towards one another. (Genesis 2:19-25)

* * * * *

When all things began, the Word already was. The Word dwelt with God, and what God was, the Word was. The Word, then, was with God at the beginning, and through him all things to be; no single thing was created without him. (John 1:1-3)

* * * * *

From among those who have been watching from the Sun Dance lodge entrance, a non-Indian woman begins yelling that the dancer is "dying," that the dance should be "stopped" immediately. Her actions annoy many, but they also endanger the vision you're now receiving. *Bishee*, Buffalo, or perhaps *Deaxkaashe*, Eagle, has come down from its watch and is guiding you on a journey. It's a journey that will guide you throughout your life. She must be quieted. An old man slowly walks to the center pole and begins to pray with his fan of eagle feathers to the mounted buffalo head and eagle. The feathers begin to pulsate. He then stands to the side of the center pole and points his feathers at the woman. The moment those feathers are pointed, the woman drops to the ground, out cold!

It must have been her excited state and the afternoon heat that caused her to fall. Her friends take her to the shade of a nearby tree, and there, try to revive her. She's out. Nothing seems to work.

* * * * *

In 1905, a 26-year-old physicist by the name of Albert Einstein proposed that light was made up of particles. He called the particles "photons," with qualities that are discrete and incremental, properties belonging to a granular universe. Photons act not unlike a stream of bullets shot from a machine gun. This proposal was proven by the photoelectric effect, i.e., electrons dislodge atoms immediately upon hitting an object. Waves have a delayed effect, taking several oscillations to occur. Einstein was awarded the Nobel Prize in 1921 for this research.

In 1926, the Austrian physicist, Erwin Schrodinger, suggested that light was made up of waves. In fact, all of nature is a great wave phenomenon. This is demonstrated when electrons are boiled off a hot tungsten filament.

The question is then asked, "How can light be made up of particles and of waves? Isn't that a contradiction?"

In 1927, the Swedish physicist, Niels Bohr, developed the "Complementarity Principle" that explained this dilemma. The mutually exclusive properties of wave and particle are not, in fact, objective properties within light. They do not belong to light. Waves and particles are properties of human interaction with light. Our participation with light creates these properties. Specifically, depending on how the experiment is set up, light can be made into waves or particles. All depends on what the observer wants to see. By extension, reality itself exists as a probability of potentialities, as a wave (or particle) function, until an interaction occurs with the human participant. At that very moment, the "collapse of the wave function" transpires--a quantum jump.

As Bohr wrote, "When it comes to atoms, language can be used only as poetry. The poet, too, is not nearly so concerned with describing facts as with creating images."

* * * * *

"May the universe in some strange sense be brought into being by the participation of those who participate?.... The vital act is the act of participation. Participation is the incontrovertible new concept given by quantum mechanics. It strikes down the term 'observer' of classical theory, the man who stands safely behind the thick glass wall and watches what goes on without taking part. It can't be done, quantum mechanics says."

So wrote the physicist, John Wheeler, in *Gravitation* (1973).

* * * * *

Because he could never use his medicine to injure another, the old man comes over to the woman. Standing over her, he "touches her up" with his feathers. She immediately awakens. And she's fine.

That woman continues to look on at the Sun Dance, but you know, she doesn't say another word all that afternoon.

What had been channeled through the cottonwood center pole and eagle feathers, what has guided you on a wondrous journey, and what had been directed at a woman who thought she stood safely outside, touched that woman! Each was unequivocally linked, if only for a moment. Each participated in the Sun Dance.

The Tower[11]

The people of your village, numbering some two thousand men, women and children, have built a massive stone wall. The wall is 2.7 meters thick, 3.2 meters high and perhaps seven hundred meters in circumference, completely enclosing the village. At one point along the wall a massive stone tower, some 10 meters in diameter, has been built. An internal flight of stairs ascends to a panoramic view of the surrounding countryside. The project took tremendous coordinated effort--planning, gathering the various materials, construction, maintenance, all of which means considerable time spent away from subsistence activities. The wall may be the first of its kind ever built. And what that wall encloses is certainly the first of its kind.

Within the walls--your people live year around, not traveling with the seasons nor following the nomadic herds of wild gazelles, goats and boars. Within the walls--your relatives engage in extensive trading with distant peoples for salt, obsidian, shells and bitumen. Within the walls--the burials include some

---

[11]For additional ethnographic background, see Fagan 1989.

bodies adorned with jewelry and buried with valuable tools while other bodies are without jewelry. Within the walls is the meager harvest of cultivated wheat and barley, stored for the winter and spring meals. The gazelle is still hunted; but you also eat of the grains you plant, harvest and store yearly. Within the walls there is a sense of protection from those from without who desire what is now within.

The time is some 9,400 years ago at a site that would later be called Jericho in the Jordan Valley.

* * * * *

For more than ninety-nine percent of its history, humanity has lived by gathering the wild plants and hunting the wild animals of the land. Beginning some 10,000 years ago all this changed. In the Hwang Ho (Yellow) River valley of China, in the Tehuacan and Oaxaca regions of Mexico, in the Nam Teng River valley of Thailand, and in the Jordan valley wild plants were domesticated. Although at slightly differing times, all these sites where domestication first took place occurred independent of each other. Millet, rice, maize, yam, wheat and barley, soon followed by dog, goat, cattle, pig and turkey, became inalterably tied to humanity. What first occurred only 10,000 years ago has dramatically altered how humanity relates to itself and to the natural world.

With the domestication of plants and animals, humanity becomes sedentary. Near the springs and along the water ways, permanent villages begin dotting the landscape where nomadic bands of people once traveled with the wild herds in their seasonal cycles. With domestication, significant craft as well as task specialization emerge. New, more function-specific, types of tools are made, helping produce a wealth of new material goods. With domestication, access to and distribution of resources is socially differentiated. Some receive more, while others receive less. Political authority is centralized. A few make the decisions for many. Social class distinctions emerge. Society is no longer egalitarian. New religious orders, such as priesthoods and temple complexes, emerge. Humanity begins to relate to the sacred in new ways.

* * * * *

Every artist is a special kind of person.

* * * * *

While not immediately significant, the human population eventually and radically increases after the domestication of plants and animals. It is important to point out that this growth in population is as much a result of the increased yield in food production as it is the requirements for increased labor input to sustain that mode and level of production. Preparing the soil, planting, irrigating, weeding, harvesting and storing the harvest necessitate intensive amounts of human labor. The increased yield allows larger families, yet larger families are needed to produce that yield. The one influences the other that influences the one.

It is estimated that 500,000 years ago, humanity numbered five million individuals throughout the inhabited world. The human population remained stable, at five million, up to the domestication of plants and animals. By 5,000 years ago, the population had grown twenty-fold to 100 million. In 1600 A.D., with the advent of the industrial revolution, the world population was 500 million. And, by 1992, in less than 400 years, the human population has grown more than ten fold to 5.5 billion people. The United Nations estimates that the world population in the year 2000 will be 6.3 billion people. Each year, a 100 million human beings are added to the world's population.

This new way of relating to the land was quickly adopted by gatherer-hunter peoples. By 2,000 years ago, domesticated farmer or herder ways of life characterized most of the world's societies and could be found in virtually every ecological niche of the earth.

As significant as domestication and all the associated changes are, as with the creation of the first stone tools, the human's conceptualization of the process and the associated changes is as significant. Some 10,000 years ago, humanity's view of the natural world was momentously altered. To domesticate, a conscious effort is required. The human deliberately interferes with the natural cycles of a plant or animal, rendering that plant or animal dependent on the human. But in the process, the human is also rendered dependent on that plant or animal. And as a result, the desired attributes of the plant or animal eventually yield higher productivity.

Domestication renders something once "wild" dependent on the human for its continued existence. Or rephrased, domestication is a measure of loss of fitness in something to survive on its own. After years of selective planting, maize seeds became larger and clustered on its cob. The yield of this food source increased as a result. But maize could no longer effectively disperse its own seeds. Humans must now do what once was done naturally. Maize can no longer survive on its own.

Domestication eventually produces higher yields in the plant or animal. The emphasis is on the "eventual." In the instance of plants, the higher yield was not the motivation for domestication. Higher yield is an eventual, though not foreseen, consequence of domestication. For hundreds of years after the domestication of plants, plants were, in fact, less productive per capita than the harvest from gathering wild plants. Given the unpredictability of seasonal climatic changes and the crude horticultural techniques available, domesticated plants were also a far less secure food source than wild plants. The quality of human health actually deteriorated immediately after the domestication of plants. The size of the human anatomy decreased. And the populations of the farming villages did not immediately increase. Gatherer-hunters always had a diversity and relative abundance of food stuffs to select from. All of their eggs were never placed in a single basket. In comparison with their gatherer-hunter neighbors, early farmers lived a very unstable and precarious existence. Why the domestication of plants was so rapidly adopted by gatherer-hunters remains a mystery to archaeologists. But eventually the yield from the plants did increase as did craft specialization, class distinctions and population.

Domestication forms a symmetrical relationship. As a plant becomes dependent on the human, the human becomes dependent on the plant. To continue to break bread together, wheat must continue to be grown. As the human population grows, the wheat harvest must necessarily grow. More natural lands must be brought under cultivation. The productivity of the domesticated plant or animal must be refined and increased. As a consequence, the domestication of the natural world extends the boundaries of the culture-created world. Humanity becomes the caretaker of an ever-increasing garden of its own creation. Hence the rise of "civilization."

As the cultural boundaries expand, there is less direct contact with the natural world, though this is certainly not apparent in the early stages of domestication. Nevertheless, domestication is as a barrier between humanity and nature. If the human garden is the domestic garden, then the natural garden is the wild garden. Domestication distinguishes between "domestic" and "wild." In the gatherer-hunter world, no such distinction is made. All plants and animals, and humans are part of a singular garden. The idea of "wildness" and "wilderness" becomes ingrained in the thinking of farmers and herders. Domestication separates the natural, the "wild," from the cultural, the "civilized."

Domestication not only separates, but it presupposes actively keeping the wild out of the cultivated fields and domestic herds. Without constant vigilance, the domestic returns to the wild. And any wild qualities that surface within the domestic must be purged. The domestic must be controlled if it is to be predictable and productive. If the domestic is the constructive and beneficial, then the "wildness" is not only something other than the cultivated, it is also an adversary of the domestic. The wild is potentially destructive of the domestic and thus harmful to the farmer or herder. Domestication attempts to control and dominate the natural, the "wild," by the cultural, the "civilized."

Domestication not only attempts to separate and control wild plants and animals, but "wildness" is extended to other humans. Those who do not cultivate the fields or herd the cattle are thought of as a potential threat and must be kept at bay. History has repeatedly portrayed the nomadic peoples as threats to farmers. But it may not have been such experiences that first categorized the nomadic peoples as wild. It may simply have been guilt-by-association. As the wild plant and wild animal is the enemy of the domestic plant and domestic animal, those who live by the wild plant and wild animal are the enemies of those who live by the domestic plant and domestic animal. As their plants and animals are wild, so too are these peoples. "Wild" peoples are separated from and dominated by the "civilized" peoples.

Within the walls of Jericho, the wilds are kept at bay and the domestic is kept under dominion.

* * * * *

"*Wilderness* n. 1. An unsettled, uncultivated region left in its natural condition, esp.: a. A large wild tract of land covered with dense vegetation or forests. b. An extensive area, as a desert or ocean, that is barren or empty; waste. c. A piece of land set aside to grow wild. 2. Something likened to a wild region in bewildering vastness, perilousness, or unchecked profusion: *a wilderness of voices.*"

The American Heritage Dictionary. Second College Edition, 1982.

* * * * *

Then God said, "Let us make man in our image and likeness to rule the fish in the sea, the birds of heaven, the cattle, all wild animals on earth, and all reptiles that crawl upon the land." So God created man in his own image; in the image of God he created him; male and female he created them. God blessed them and said to them, "Be fruitful and increase, fill the earth and subdue it, rule over the fish in the sea, the birds of heaven, and every living thing that moves upon the earth." God also said, "I give you all plants that bear seed everywhere on earth, and every tree bearing fruit which yields seed: they shall be yours for food." (Genesis 1:26-29)

* * * * *

When the Lord God made earth and heaven, there was neither shrub nor plant growing wild upon the earth, because the Lord God had sent no rain on the earth; nor was there any man to till the ground. A mist used to rise out of the earth and water all the surface of the ground. Then the Lord God formed a man from the dust of the ground and breathed into his nostrils the breath of life. Thus the man became a living creature. Then the Lord God planted a garden in Eden away to the east, and there he put the man whom he had formed. The Lord God made trees pleasant to look at and good for food; and in the middle of the garden he set the tree of life and the tree of knowledge of good and evil. (Genesis 2:5-9)

* * * * *

The Lord God took the man and put him in the garden of Eden to till it and care for it. He told the man, "You may eat from every tree in the garden, but not from the tree of the knowledge of good and evil; for on the day that you eat from it, you will certainly die." (Genesis 2:15-17)

* * * * *

The serpent was more crafty than any wild creature that the Lord God had made. He said to the woman, "Is it true that God has forbidden you to eat from any tree of the garden?" The woman answered the serpent, "We may eat the fruit of any tree in the garden, except the tree in the middle of the garden; God has forbidden us either to eat or to touch the fruit of that; if we do, we shall die." The serpent said, "Of course you will not die. God knows that as soon as you eat it, your eyes will be opened and you will be like God knowing both good and evil." When the woman saw that the fruit of the tree was good to eat, and that it was pleasing to the eye and tempting to contemplate, she took some and ate it. She also gave her husband some and he ate it. Then the eyes of both of them were opened and they discovered that they were naked; so they stitched fig-leaves together and made themselves loincloths. (Genesis 3:1-7)

* * * * *

The Lord God made tunics of skins for Adam and his wife and clothed them. He said, "The man has become like one of us, knowing good and evil; what if he now reaches out his hand and takes fruit from the tree of life also, eats it and lives for ever?" So the Lord God drove him out of the garden of Eden to till the ground from which he had been taken. He cast him out, and to the east of the garden of Eden he stationed the cherubim and a sword whirling and flashing to guard the way to the tree of life. (Genesis 3:21-24)

* * * * *

"*Wilderness* in Greek refers to a "desolate, deserted, lonely place," a "desert." In this sense, wilderness can be delineated as the absence of relationships. "The Fall" is comprised of the demise of relationship between the Creator and the created, human to human, man and woman, humans and nature. In its purest form "wilderness" is where humans have not established their dominion and are therefore subject to forces which threaten to take dominion over him. It is there that he/she learns the truth of their poverty and vulnerability and must look outside him/herself to find meaning and security, to find relationship with the Creator, and through the Creator, find relationship with nature and with humans. We cannot within ourselves reconcile any of these relationships, BUT our God can and will. 'The Lord will surely comfort Zion and will look with compassion on all her ruins; he will make her deserts (wilderness) like Eden, her wastelands like the garden of the Lord. Joy and gladness will be found in her, thanksgiving and the sound of singing' (Isaiah 51:3)."

So spoke the pastor Dr. Richard Irish in his presentation to the *Wilderness Seminar* in February of 1992.

* * * * *

And you look down from your steel tower onto the forests below. With binoculars in hand, you watch for smoke, and observe the movement and size of the herds and the condition of their habitat. It's your responsibility.

It's a vast natural resource that needs protecting. Homes are to be built and jobs provided. And with the information you provide, the Fish and Game Department will be able to issue the proper number of elk tags.

Soul Food[12]

You last piece of soap stone is brought out. With eyes focused, the stone is held in hand under the flickering light of the oil lamp. It's turned this way, then that, catching the eye and the light in the contours of the stone. Who's within the stone, to be released as the stone is chipped away? Held under the flickering light..., it's her! There's no mistaking it. It's Sedna, she who lives at the bottom of the sea! And the hands become busy. With steel axe and knife, the stone covering is carefully removed from Sedna. The chips fly from and fall to the floor of the igloo. In no time, the image of Sedna is released from the soap stone and held close in hand.

* * * * *

The world is an empty place....
All is dark..
There is nothing,
       flat earth in all directions.
There are no animals,
         no seals,
             no fishes,
                  no birds.
All is empty,...
       earth everywhere.
There are two men.

---

[12]The story text is from the Iglulik and Netsilik Inuit, two central Eskimo people. This account is similar to that found throughout the oral literature of all Eskimo peoples. For additional ethnographic background, see Nelson 1983, Rasmussen 1929 and 1931, and Speck 1935.

They are already full-grown when they came from the ground.
They live together there,
        but it is not a very satisfactory life...
With the words of a song,..[13]
        they sing.
        "A human being here
                A penis here.
        May its opening be wide
                And roomy.
        Opening,
                opening,
                        opening..."
These are the words they sing..
One of the men is turned into a woman,
        she is soon with child...
From these three come the peoples of the earth,...
        though some children are found in the earth.
A girl child,
        she can be found near the camps,
                without much searching.
A boy child,...
        you must journey far,
                with much difficulty,
                        to find him in the earth....

---

[13]In order to convey a sense of the oral nuance of those stories emanating out of an oral-based tradition, I have re-formatted these story texts in a "poetic style." The resulting endeavor tries to retain some of the dramatic rhythms and pacing. Identified within each text are groupings of morpheme clusters or "verses" separated by pauses of varying lengths which are marked with commas and periods. Approach oral-based texts as a performance event and not as a reading from a fixed object on a page. Each text presented here is based upon a re-telling I have performed in class, inspired by a traditional narrative. The source of the original story text is identified in a corresponding footnote and the Bibliography.

The camps of people grow.
Life is hard.....
The people have no animals to hunt,
          people live by eating the earth.....
There are only so many ways you can prepare a meal with
earth!..
The people move about,
          they camp,
                    they break up the soil for their food.
Their clothes are bad,
          full of holes..
Their kayaks are no good,
          full of holes as well.
They sink in the water!...
Their summer tents are bad,
          as the wind always blows through.
They have no seal oil to heat their igloos in the cold winter,
          no oil to give light in the dark winter,
                    no oil to cook their earth food.
It's a hard life.....
There is one thing the people have....
They have no fear!..
They do not live by,.
          endangering the souls of others!
They fear nothing....
In the camp there is a beautiful girl.
She is named Sedna...
She is a hard worker,
          can prepare the soil for eating with the best of them!
She is desired by many young men.
They come to marry,
          but each is turned down.
She is very particular....
One day a handsome bird arrives in camp.
He wants Sedna...

He gives promises of a good life,
> tents without holes,
>> warm clothes,...
>>> good food.
Sedna hears these words of the bird,
> she joins this bird....
Together they fly off to the land to the north...
What Sedna finds in the camp of the bird,
> is bad.
The tents have holes,
> the clothes are bad,
>> the soil is no good!..
Her husband,...
> he is no good as well.
He spends his time gambling with the other birds,...
> pays her no attention.
Tears fill the eyes of Sedna....
Sedna's father decides to pay her a visit.
He travels north with his dog,
> in his kayak.
He arrives,
> he sees his daughter.
The birds are out gambling.
The father puts Sedna in his kayak,
> they head back to their camp....
The birds return,
> find their Sedna gone..
They fly high in the sky,
> look in all the directions.
They see her down there,
> fly toward the kayak..
They hover just above the kayak,
> small in the water,
>> the power of their wings causes great waves to
>> form in the open sea..

At any moment the boat will capsize,
      they will be lost....
The father fears for his life,
      he knowing what the birds want.
The father throws Sedna into the sea...
She can not swim,
      she grabs hold of the side of the kayak.
The father pulls out his knife,
      he cuts off the first joints of Sedna's fingers.
At that moment something happens....
The flesh,
      the bone of Sedna's fingers hits the water,
          they are fishes of all kinds,
             seals,..
                walrus..
Sedna has a second set of finger joints,
      she continues to hold tight to the kayak.
The knife cuts away.
The flesh,
      the bone hit the water,
          caribou,..
             bear,.
                wolves roam the land...
Sedna grabs to the kayak with the last of her fingers.
The birds hover close.
The knife cuts.
Birds of all kinds,
      all the other animals come forth from the earth...
Without fingers,
      Sedna falls to the bottom of the sea.
The birds leave.
The father has saved his life....
He makes his way back to the land,
      sets up a camp....
From the bottom of the sea,
      Sedna makes her way to the land.

She is very disappointed in dad!..
That night Sedna comes into her father's camp,...
        she kills that old man,
             she kills his dog.....
The ground opens up,
        the three fall to the bottom of the sea..
That's where they are now...
Sedna is the spirit of all the sea animals.
She lives at the bottom of the sea,
        in an igloo that opens to the above world,
             she can see everything...
She sits there on fine furs.
On one side of her,
        a spring of fresh water flows all the time.
On the other side,
        a lamp that lights the inside of her igloo...
In the dark reaches of the igloo,
        the father is ready to,...
             grab at you...
The dog is out there,
        ready to bite.
It's a dangerous place,
        huge rocks roll about that can crush...
There is an abyss that must be crossed,
        if you are to enter Sedna's igloo....
The people become great hunters.
They hunt the caribou,
        the walrus,
             the seals..
The seals give warm clothing,
        coverings for tents that keep the wind out,
           tools of bone,
                tools of ivory...

From the seal come our kayaks,
    and umiaks that don't sink in the sea,
        oil to light the darkness,
           oil to heat the cold winter.
The people eat meat...
They no longer live,
    by eating the earth.

* * * * *

"Most high, omnipotent, good Lord,
    Thine are all praise, glory, honor and all benedictions.
To Thee alone, Most High, do they belong
    And no man is worthy to name Thee.
Praise be to Thee, My Lord, with all Thy creatures,
    Especially Brother Sun,
    Who is our day and lightens us therewith.
Beautiful is he and radiant with great splendor;
    Of Thee, Most High, he bears expression.
Praise be to Thee, my Lord, for Sister Moon,
    and for the stars
    In the heavens which Thou has formed bright, precious
    and fair.
Praise be to Thee, my Lord, for Brother Wind,
    And for the air and the cloud of fair and all weather
    Through which Thou givest sustenance to Thy creatures.
Praise be, my Lord, for Sister Water.
    Who is most useful, humble, precious and chaste.
Praise be, my Lord, for Brother Fire,
    By whom Thou lightest up the night:
He is beautiful, merry, robust and strong.
Praise be, my Lord, for our sister Mother Earth,
    Who sustains and governs us
    And brings forth diverse fruits with many-hued flowers
    and grass."
So wrote Frances of Assisi (1181-1226) in his *Canticle of Brother Sun, Sister Moon.*

* * * * *

But there is one other thing the people have that they didn't have before. Now they live by endangering the souls of others. Now the people have fear! Before Sedna, the people didn't have fear. But why should the people have fear?

We must ask what it is that the people hunt? That which they hunt is made from whom?

The people hunt the animals made from the flesh and bone of Sedna. The people eat of the body that is from Sedna. And, as Sedna had a soul, did not the animals also receive souls?

* * * * *

Helping Spirit, *Issitoq*, Giant Eye
(drawing by shaman)

Soon after his parents had died, an Iglulik man was visited by this melancholy spirit, *Issitoq*. It said to him, "You must not be afraid of me, for I too struggle with sad thoughts; therefore I will go with you and be your helping spirit." Its specialty is finding people who have broken respect rules and taboos.

* * * * *

There's a young girl who's foolish,
            she's with child,
                        not married....
She leaves camp alone,
            lets the unformed child go from within her..

On the ice,
      the body of the child is dead....
The girl returns to camp,
      no one learns of her misdeed..
The dogs are always hungry,
      they come along,
            they eat the flesh of the child....
The body is dead,
      its soul remains.
Among the dogs,
      the soul is as a dog,
          travels with them.
It's a bad life,
      that of a dog,
         little food,
             always fighting amongst themselves....
It happens that the dogs come close to the waters,
      the soul of the child goes among the seals,
         becomes one of them....
It likes the life of the seal,
      plenty of food,
         always playing with one another...
The child's soul is restless.
It moves among the walrus,
      becomes one of them....
But they are a lazy animal,
      always battling themselves with their huge snouts....
The child's soul moves among the caribou,
      becomes one of them....
But they are forever roaming about for food,
      food of moss,
         grass!...
The soul of the child returns among the seal.
It's a good life.....
One day as the seal is swimming about,
      a man in a kayak paddles over head....

The seal knows that the wife of this man is without child...
The seal allows himself to be caught..
When the wife takes in the flesh of the seal,
      she takes in the soul of the child...
She soon learns of a child within her,
      and gives birth to a beautiful son...
The boy has a wondrous ability,
      no one knows why....
He can speak the languages of the dog,
      of the walrus,
          of the caribou,
             of the seal..
He becomes a great hunter....

* * * * *

As Sedna is our kinsmen, so too are the animals, in body and in soul. When we hunt the animal, are we not living by endangering the souls of our kinsmen? When we eat of their flesh, are we not eating of ours?

As with all kinsmen, the people enter into an exchange with the animals.[14] The hunter never tries to take the animal in the hunt, but instead offers it a gift. If the gift is judged worthy, the animal will offer itself up to the hunter. The animal, on its own, gives itself freely to the hunter. That which the animal gives is, after all, only its body, and not that which gives life and is most important, its soul.

The gifts given to the animals are offerings of respect. Dogs are not to chew on the bones of animals. Mittens of caribou fur are to be mended only at certain times of the year. When a seal offers itself up to the hunter, it does so for a drink of fresh water. The fresh water must be given. One hunts what one needs to

---

[14]This Inuit animal-hunter relationship reflects a pervasive and predominate North American indigenous attitude, i.e., you give before you can receive from the animal and you hunt only what you can use and use all that you hunt. "Use" is defined in terms of family sustenance and not excess.

hunt, never taking more than the family can use. And the taboos, ways of respecting the animal, go on.

Having given its body in the hunt, the soul of the animal remains in the camp of the hunter, watching the actions of the people for three days. If respect is shown, the soul of the animal returns to Sedna. There at the bottom of the sea, Sedna places a new body on the soul of the animal. And the animal goes on.

However, if the soul returns without the respect it's due, it returns with larvae, worms and mites. In turn, the impurities gather in the hair of Sedna and, having no fingers to remove these annoyances, they continue to accumulate and grow. It does not take long for Sedna to become angry. When this happens, she no longer places bodies on the returning souls. Without bodies to hunt, the people are without meat to eat, oil to heat and hides to clothe themselves. The people suffer for what was not given the souls of animals. Sedna is to be feared, for she controls life itself.

When respect has not been given, the animals and Sedna withhold that which the people need, and the balance must be restored. In a specially-built igloo that holds the entire camp, the people gather around and sing the words of the shaman's songs.

* * * * *

The great sea stirs me.
The great sea sets me adrift,
       it sways me like the weed on a river-stone.

The sky's height stirs me.
The strong wind blows through my mind.
It carries me with it,
       so I shake with joy.

Earth and the great weather move me,
      have carried me away
          and move my inward parts with joy.
(Uvavnuk, an Iglulik woman)

* * * * *

Soon the air is filled with words and the helping spirits of the shaman. The shaman dances about. And then it happens; the shaman's soul leaves his body, and the body dies. A most difficult journey takes place. The soul of the shaman travels to the bottom of the sea to the abode of Sedna. Challenges await at every point. He must watch for the huge boulders that roll about. He must cross the abyss. And then there is the old man and his dog. He must avoid their grasp. There are dangers to be avoided.

Standing before Sedna, the shaman must remove the impurities infesting her hair. If he is successful with all of these challenges, the shaman must promise that the people who have not shown respect will, along with all the people, now show the respect due their kinsmen. If Sedna agrees, she will again start placing bodies on the souls of animals. The shaman returns among the people, his body alive again, as the songs continue. Then all present, one by one, speak of the taboos each may have broken. The words reiterate to all what it is that must be given in exchange for what can be received.

* * * * *

Go and ask the cattle, ask the birds of the air to inform you, or tell the creatures that crawl to teach you, and the fishes of the sea to give you instruction. Who cannot learn from all these that the Lord's own hand has done this? In God's hand are the souls of all that live, the spirits of all human kind. (Job 12:7-10)

* * * * *

It's been a difficult winter for your family. Not many seals have offered themselves up to the hunters. The wind blows a cold wind today, and the children and the elders need the warmth of the food and oil the seal could offer. So, with harpoon in one hand and the stone image of Sedna in the other, you go to the ice and the breathing holes of the seal. Words are given.

Beast of the Sea,
Come and offer yourself in the dear early morning!
Beast of the plain!
Come and offer yourself in the dear morning!

It's a long wait. Watching, without moving, with harpoon ready. Then something stirs in the water. A seal comes forth for a breath of air..., and some fresh water!

* * * * *

Shaman's Journey
(inspired by a drawing by Jessie Oonark 1970)

A Plant[15]

Following your topographic maps of a forested region in northern Idaho, you've come to a grassy meadow. It'll be a good place to rest. The heavy backpack is taken off and the soft grasses make a good bed. As fingers slide through the blades of grass, they come upon the plant. It's plucked from the ground, roots attached and held close for viewing.

* * * * *

Walking past the village blacksmith's shop, the pleasant ring of hammers striking an anvil catches your attention. It's music in harmony. Going into the shop, you find that the lower notes that you hear are produced by heavy hammers, while the higher notes are caused by lighter hammers striking on the anvil. As you've observed from the strings of a musical instrument, the objects creating the sounds can be broken down into discrete, mathematical units. Each of these units, when paired with another that has been divided into exact parts of two, three or four, will produce a harmonious sound. A string is stretched tight and plucked. A sound, a note, is heard. A second string, exactly half as long as the first, is stretched along side the first and plucked. The sound of the note is an octave above the first note. A third string, exactly one third as long as the first, is stretched and plucked. The sound is a fifth above the first. It's all harmony to your ears. But when the second and third strings are shortened or lengthened, if only slightly, the plucked sound is discordant. The world of sound is governed by a universal and all pervading mathematics, numbers in balance and harmony.

You are Pythagoras (580-497 B.C.), and what you assert for the world of sound you assert for all of the world. The world of shapes and forms are governed by a harmony of exact numbers. Knowledge of this fundamental relationship between the world of

---

[15]For additional background, see Barfield 1957, Bronowski 1973, Hall 1983, Matthews 1978 and Nasr 1968.

space and mathematics leads you, Pythagoras, to a critical discovery.

* * * * *

Let us replicate in our own experience what Pythagoras discovered in the 6th century B.C.   We'll begin with the assumption that gravity is vertical and that horizontal stands at a right angle to it.   The conjunction of the vertical and the horizontal fixes a right angle. Following Pythagoras, this basic spatial relationship is to be found throughout all of nature. From this assumption a most important observation and subsequent application can be made. An experiment will demonstrate.

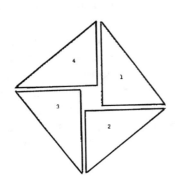

Take a right angle and cut it out from a piece of paper in the form of a triangle.   Lay it down on another piece of paper, and with the side opposite the right angle facing out, move it down and sideways four times.   As the triangle is moved, place the sides of the right angle against each other. Draw   a   line   completely around   the   sides   of   the triangle. After moving the right angle four times, the triangle should rest at its original starting place. A square is formed if the hypotenuse of the right angle is kept on the outside as it is moved, i.e., a square of the hypotenuse. Only a right angle can do this.

Because of the right angle, two other squares can be formed from the movement of the same triangle. On the same piece of paper that the previous square was drawn, place the hypotenuse of the triangle against the outside of the square. Draw a line along the sides of the right angle. Now place the triangle on the outside of the adjacent side of the square, again with the hypotenuse against the square. Draw around the sides of the right angle of the triangle. Each of the two sides of the right angle should mark out each of two separate squares, though each smaller than the original square.

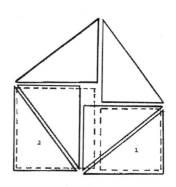

From this experiment and with these observations, a general theorem can be stated for every triangle that contains a right angle: the square on the hypotenuse is equal to the square on one of the other sides plus the square of the other. This is true, if and only if, the angle they contain is a right angle. Of course, this is the Pythagorean theorem, i.e., a right angle is the square of the hypotenuse equal to the sum of the squares on the other two sides.

The test of the theorem offers proof of its validity. If a triangle is 5 inches by 4 inches by 3 inches, for instance, is it a right angle? Five inches is the hypotenuse and squared it is 25. Four inches squared is 16, and three inches squared is 9. The sum of these two squares is equal to the square of the hypotenuse, i.e., 25. The triangle contains a right angle, and our theorem has validity based upon this test.

$$a^2 + b^2 = c^2$$

For Pythagoras, the world of space is governed by exact numbers. Within nature and throughout the cosmos, numbers organize the forms, structures and dimensions of all being into a *harmonium*, "harmony." As with the music of a properly stringed instrument, the parts of the cosmos "vibrate" in harmony. In turn, particular combinations of numbers have greater significance for Pythagoras. One such combination is the *tetractys*, "source and root of everlasting nature," a triangle made up of ten dots. The number ten is consequently a sacred number. Another combination is the number four, which represents "justice."

```
        .
      .   .
    .   .   .
  .   .   .   .
```

This is not to suggest that all is in harmony. Much of the physical world as well as our own bodies are discordant and unbalanced. In fact, the soul is condemned to a cycle of purgings in Hades and rebirths as a prisoner of the physical body. It is for this reason that Pythagoras abstained from consuming the meat of an animal. The soul of a relative could be within.

But as pure mathematical patterns are apprehended through observation and disciplined mediation by humanity, humanity can then apply these universal principles to bring order to the world and thereby redeem the self and the soul. Once harmony between one's soul and the cosmos is obtained, the soul ceases the cycles of reincarnation into varied material forms and becomes forever part of the singular divine cosmos.

While the sacred connotation of numbers has been discarded over the centuries, the monumental significance of Pythagoras's discovery of the relationship of discrete numbers to the patterns of the world continues to reverberate. As was subsequently echoed by Galileo and, later, Jacob Bronowski (1973), a contemporary philosopher of science, "the language of nature is mathematics." With this fundamental knowledge of the structure and workings of the world, geometry and physics became a science. The Doric temple of Parthenon and the Sears Building in Chicago could be built. A man could walk on the moon. With this knowledge our modern world came into being.

* * * * *

In 150 A.D., Claudius Ptolemy applied a geometric model to the heavens. Spheres and perfect circles formed the basis of his hypothesis of the planetary movements in a geocentric cosmology.

In the center of the cosmos is the Earth, in a state of rest, inclusive of both man and god. Out from the divine center, the Moon rotates in a perfect circle around the Earth. Next out is Mercury, which rotates in an epicycle, a circular rotation whose center forms the circumference that in turn circles the earth. Venus is next out, also with its own circular orbit that circles the earth. Then comes the Sun, with a simple rotation around the earth. Mars, Jupiter and Saturn follow. The finite universe is bounded by the Stars, fixed in stationary positions. As with the center of the cosmos, spirit emanates throughout all the universe, within all the celestial bodies. The driving force of each planet's rotation through the cosmos is, in fact, its soul.

Based on the principles of geometry, the Ptolemaic theory is a complex model. But it works, more or less. The appearances are accounted for, and the essences are given meaning. All of the cosmos, god and man, has its place.

The Ptolemaic Cosmos

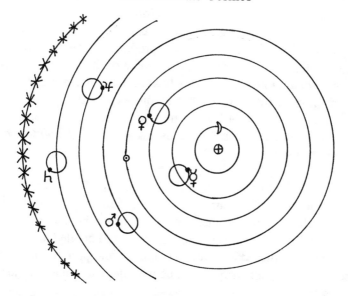

Ptolemy wrote down his hypothesis in a thirteen-volume book, *Almagest* (Syntaxis mathematica). Translated into Arabic in the 9th century, it was a standard reference work on issues of astronomy until the 16th century, for both European and Islamic astronomers.

* * * * *

From the hill overlooking the village, you look out into the heavens. Your view is crisp and clear. In the dark of the night, the Planets shine bright...and You shine bright, perfect souls in perfect orbits in perfect harmony.

* * * * *

In 1413, the first Spanish ships began raiding the coast of West Africa, taking cargo and capturing slaves from Arab traders. This was now possible because of the knowledge a new technology brought. The compass and sextant made distant navigation possible. The world was being very closely observed, and some people greatly benefitted from this new knowledge.

* * * * *

The Roman Catholic Pope asked a distinguished churchman and intellectual from Poland to reform the rather complex calendar. His name was Nicolaus Copernicus (1473-1543). Copernicus investigated an idea, first proposed in the 3rd century B.C., that placed the sun right in the middle of the universe, with the earth rotating around it. This heliocentric system was based on a much more mathematically rigorous explanation. Man was no longer the center of the cosmos. At the age of seventy, Copernicus reluctantly published his research, *The Revolution of the Heavenly Orbs*.

* * * * *

In 1517, the Protestant Reformation began. The authority of the Roman Catholic Church was being seriously challenged. After much struggle, Rome would no longer be the primary interpreter and disseminator of theological knowledge. The Reformation affirmed everyone's right to interpret for him or herself. In time, authority would be with the individual, not just the clergy.

* * * * *

Two great men were born in the year 1564. They were
William Shakespeare in England and Galileo Galilei in Italy.
Each would have quite differing but very significant influences.

In 1609, Galileo perfected an instrument for making distant
objects appear larger, as if close at hand. His telescope allowed
him to observe what human eyes had never before seen, e.g., sun
spots and Jupiter's moons. He also improved upon the
compound microscope, making minute objects appear larger. The
natural world was not only being seen, but being seen in new
ways.

Galileo further refined the model of the Copernican
heliocentric universe and fully articulated an entirely new way of
knowing the world. Based upon his observations and his
theories, Galileo maintained that the universe was a physical
universe and that the Copernican universe was "proven fact," the
truth and the only true theory of the physical universe.

It was these assertions that got Galileo into trouble with the
Cardinals of the Roman Catholic Church. He was confined to his
villa and found it difficult to publish his research. The Church
did not so much object to his theory of a heliocentric cosmos.
They in fact encouraged all theories. What the Church objected
to was a theory that maintained that all other theories were wrong
and that there was no place for a divine center in the cosmos nor
of a divine presence of any kind.

Prior to Galileo, all theory was understood as hypothesis, as
assumptions about the appearances of the cosmos. Most
critically, theory sought to account for the essences, the inner
forms behind those appearances. It did not necessarily attempt
to describe the overt and material expressions of the world.
Theory was an analogy, and not a literal representation of the
cosmos; and it was a proposition that could accommodate
differing propositions. The theory of Ptolemy was such a theory,
a theory that "saved the appearances." It was a theory that
emanated out of a Platonic world view.

Galileo, however, offered a new theory on the nature of

theory, a new epistemology. A Platonic view of the world was no longer possible. In 1632, his research was finally published (in Switzerland), *Dialogues Concerning the Two Chief World Systems*, followed in 1638 (in Holland) by *The New Science*.

* * * * *

Isaac Newton (1642-1727) offered a new theory of inertia. He schooled himself in mathematics, later inventing what is now called calculus. His conception of the universe was published in 1687, the *Principia* (*Mathematical Principles of Natural Philosophy*), and described an orderly world subsumed under a single set of laws. Following the observations suggested by Galileo, Newton's First Law of Motion states that an object at rest will remain stationary unless acted upon by some outside force, and an object in motion will continue in motion in a straight line and at a constant velocity, unless acted upon by some outside force.

The Second Law of Motion states that the acceleration of an object is directly related to the force exerted upon the object. The more force exerted, the faster the object moves. The less force exerted, the slower the object moves. And the acceleration of an object is inversely related to the mass of the object. The force exerted on an object of large mass will result in less acceleration than the same force exerted upon an object of smaller mass.

The Third Law of Motion states that for every action there is an equal and opposite reaction. No force may be exerted upon any body that does not affect a second body. From these universal laws of gravitation, Newton calculated the movement of the planets around the sun as well as the movement of an apple from a tree. The gravitational pull of the sun or the earth is inversely proportional to the square of a planet's or an apple's distance from the sun or the earth.

What applies in the solar system applies in one's back yard.

For the first time in human history, a concise and rigorous theory was proposed that maintained that the physical universe can continue movement indefinitely without an animate or a divine power regulating it. The universe is an orderly and predictable universe, governed by great mechanical forces. These forces are implicit within the autonomous laws of the universe, laws that are as absolute as that which they govern, i.e., space and time. And these are laws that are knowable by man, to be observed and used by man.

* * * * *

"A wilderness, in contrast with those areas where man and his works dominate the landscape, is hereby recognized as an area where the earth and its community of life are untrammeled by man, where man himself is a visitor who does not remain. An area of wilderness is further defined to mean in this Act an area of undeveloped Federal land retaining its primeval character and influence, without permanent improvements or human habitation, which is protected and managed so as to preserve its natural conditions and which (1) generally appears to have been affected primarily by the forces of nature, with the imprint of man's work substantially unnoticeable; (2) has outstanding opportunities for solitude or primitive and unconfined type of recreation; (3) has at least five thousand acres of land or is of sufficient size as to make practicable its preservation and use in an unimpaired condition; and (4) may also contain ecological, geological, or other features of scientific, educational, scenic, or historical value."

Wilderness Act, Act of September 3, 1964 (P.L. 88-577, 78 Stat. 890; 16 U.S.C. 1121 (note). 1131-1136).

* * * * *

The stem is 18 inches in length and is dense with scarlet colored clusters of bracts and leaves. At the tip of the stem is a tubular-shaped, yellowish-green flower, one inch in length. Examination of its roots indicates that they have not only penetrated the soil for water and nutrients such as nitrogen, but also the root tissues of the surrounding sagebrush. The plant is a semiparasitic, dependent on other plants for a portion of its nutrients. Yet, through photosynthesis, this plant helps provide what is essential for the life of others, what others depend upon.

Utilizing radiant energy and soil nutrients, the chlorophyll in its cells manufactures carbohydrates from carbon dioxide and water to release the oxygen you're now breathing. It is *Castilleja linarieaefolia* Benth., Indian Paintbrush, representing one of over 250,000 species of Angiosperms.

After a reading of the compass and a review of the map, the backpack is put on and the hike continues.

A Flower[16]

The sun points the way. You're traveling the "high country" of northern Idaho and have just come over a hill flanked by thick lodgepole pine on either side. It's been a long journey, a journey that has taken much effort to reach this certain place. There, in a small clearing of grass, the red of its petals shines bright in the sun's light.

* * * * *

Along with a host of others, you've left the camp, leaving behind the women and the uninitiated and all vestiges of the mundane, your spears and carrying bags, and your social names. You're on a solemn journey to your birth place. Single file, without a sound, you and the others walk in awe. Although it's not far into the desert, few ever visit without invitation.

Your group has arrived, and all immediately begin to clear the ground of the debris and stones that have accumulated since last you were here. The area of some twenty paces is laid smooth. Several go to a nearby rock outcropping and, from the cache, bring out with great care the churinga boards. Some are as long as an arm, most much shorter, all of wood, each richly carved with the signs of the clan ancestors and of their adventures. Sitting in a circle on the cleared earth, the churingas

---

[16]For additional background, see Bell 1983, Berndt and Berndt 1977, Emerson 1985, Frey 1987, Plato 1968, Spencer and Gillen 1899 and 1904, Stanner 1959-63, Strehlow 1947, Thoreau 1960 and Tonkinson 1978.

are passed to each of your group in turn. Each holds the oval-shaped boards close, rubbing them against himself.

A couple of the older men begin opening the veins of their arms, letting the life within fall upon the smoothed ground and upon a few other men who sit to one side of the circle. It's a gift of blood. When blood fell from the veins of the ancestors, human sons emerged out of the ground. Song has begun; the words of the ancestors, their names, their birth places, and their adventures are heard in verse. Upon the base of blood is added the white of down feathers and of pipe-clay, and the reds and yellows of clay ochres. The patterning of feather and ochre is as the designs on the churinga boards; and the ground and the men are no longer who they may have been. As the sun sets, a fire is lit. The songs continue. All sense of ordinary time and place is replaced.

* * * * *

Ground Painting
of the Wallunqua (Snake) Totem
(Warramunga Tribe, 2 meters long)

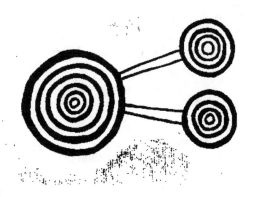

In the flickering light of the stars and the fire, those who are painted will dance out the adventures of the ancestors. And the ancestors have emerged. It's they who move about in their ancient landscape. Those who have journeyed have journeyed far, as you now will witness and participate in the *Alcheringa*, the Dreamtime.

* * * * *

The earth is a barren plain...
There are no mountains,.
     no rivers,.
          no animals,.
               no plants...
It's a dry plain,.
     without light..
All is in perpetual darkness,.
     without form...
Night oppresses the earth.....
There's no life,.
     no beginning,.
          there's no death...
The sun,.
     the moon,.
          the animals,.
               the plants,.
     all are resting in a state of half-dream,.
     under the earth,.
          in a perpetual eternity...
They do not stir.....
On the surface,
     scattered about,...
          are half-developed infants..
They do not grow,
     they do not die..
All exist in a perpetual eternity....
Karora is one of those in perpetual sleep.

On the earth that covers him,
  is a bed of red,
    of purple flowers.
Near his head towers a churinga pole.
Below this surface of flowers,
  of churinga,
    lies the bandicoot ancestor....
Without warning,
  all over the earth,
    the awakening happens..
Karora begins to think,
  to desire,
    and from his navel,
      from his armpits,
        bandicoots burst through the
        earth,
          and spring to life....
Now Karora himself breaks through the crust of earth,
  the place where he had laid becomes a soak,
    filled with the sweet dark juice of the
    honeysuckle buds..
All over,
  the ancestors emerge from the ground,
    born out of their own eternity...
They are the kangaroo,
  the emu,
    the opossum,
      the crocodile,
        the moon,
          the wallaby,
  some are men,
    some are women,
  all are in various shapes,
    various appearances.

They are human,
       they are animal,...
              as one....
The sun floods the land in light.....
Slowly the eyelids of Karora open.
He is yet not fully awake,
       he thinks,
              he hungers...
All about him is a mass of bandicoots.
Two are taken.
With the heat of the sun as fire,
       he cooks,
              he eats these bandicoots....
His thoughts now turn to a helpmate.
The sun hides its face under a veil of hair-string pendants,
       vanishes.
Karora falls asleep...
While asleep,
       from the armpit of Karora,
              emerges a bull-roarer,
                     that which gives voice to the
                     ancestors...
In one night,
       the bull-roarer grows to a full-grown young man,
              the firstborn son..
When Karora awakes,
       he sees his son lying beside him.
Dawn breaks....
The son awakes,
       he dances around his father,
              the father sits adorned in his ceremonial
              designs of down feathers,
                     of blood.
The first ceremony is held.....
That day the son kills some bandicoots.
They had been playing peacefully.

The meat is cooked under the sun's heat.
Karora,
      his son eat the meat of the bandicoots...
The sun passes,
      sleep falls upon Karora,
            his son..
As Karora sleeps,
      two more sons are born out of his armpits.
The dance is held....
This happens for many days,
      many nights,..
            soon there are many sons born out of Karora...
The many sons have a great hunger,
      and soon devour all the bandicoots,
            they who had themselves sprung from Karora...

* * * * *

Painting from Aryes Rock
(7 meters in length)

* * * * *

In their hunger,
        Karora sends his sons on a long hunt,
           to search for food.
There is tall grasses,
        trees,
           the sons search for the bandicoots.
In the great expanse,
        no bandicoots are found,
           the sons return to Karora,..
               hungry,.
                  tired....
Suddenly,
        a sound comes to the ears of Karora,
           to the ears of his many sons.
It is a sound like that which comes from the whirling of the
bull-roarer...
Karora,
        his sons search for the sound,
           stabbing at all the bandicoot nests with their
           sticks..
They search,
        they search...
Something darts up,.
        is gone....
It is a sandhill wallaby.
The sons throw sticks,
        hit the wallaby,
           break its leg.
It limps off giving words in song,
        "I've grown lame.
        I'm a man as you are,
           not a bandicoot!" it sings....
Karora,
        the bandicoot brothers return to their soak,
           they sit at its edge in a circle...

From the east,

      comes a great flood of sweet honey from the
      honeysuckle buds,...

           washes the bandicoot ancestors back into the
           soak...

The rocks,

      the stones that you now see scattered about the soak
      are the undying bodies of the bandicoot brothers.

At the bottom of the soak lies,...

      Karora himself,

          fast asleep.....

* * * * *

As happened at the soak of Karora, after many adventures
and misadventures, an overpowering weariness falls upon all of
the ancestors. And the ancestors return to the earth. But that is
not the end of the Dreamtime. The ancestors have left much
behind and even now are still present. Mountains and rivers, fire
and the moon, animals and humans, various ceremonials, and
death itself are now present on the earth's surface.

Like Karora, the spirit of each ancestor is at his or her resting
site: a soak, a rock outcropping, a river's bank. Karora remains
at his soak. The entire landscape abounds with these sacred sites.
These are the ceremonial places, the places of initiation and of
honoring the ancestors, the birth places of the ancestors and of
the human descendants of those ancestors.

At each of these sacred sites are kept the churinga boards.
Within each carved board is the spirit of the kindred ancestor.
Karora's spirit is within his churinga boards.

Each ancestor vested his or her spirit in the particular animal
or plant that came from his or her body. The bandicoot seen
nesting in the nearby thicket has the spirit of Karora within it.
All of the life and all of the landscape we now view is inundated
with the spirits of the ancestors.

* * * * *

Kangaroo
(Oenpelli Tribe, bark-painting 29" high)

* * * * *

The ancestors also left the knowledge of the Dreamtime to their human descendants. In the words in song and story, in the actions of ceremonial procedures and in the designs of the churingas, the ways of maintaining the proper relationship with the ancestor and the Dreamtime world are made accessible. In the words, ceremonials and designs are also the spirits of the ancestors. Karora has his particular songs and stories, his ceremonials and designs.

And the spirit of each ancestor is within the human descendants of that ancestor. The human descendants, who share in this kinship, are organized into social clan groupings. The human clan of Karora is the Bandicoot clan, having its own sacred site, churinga boards, songs and ceremonials, and animal kinsmen--the bandicoot. Each is intimately tied in spirit to Karora, their source of life and meaning.

Because of this animal-human kinship, clan members do not eat of their own animal kinsmen. It would be as eating of oneself. But among the various clans, reciprocity predominates, and each shares in the animal kinsmen of other clans. The Bandicoot clan members can eat of the kangaroo, while the Kangaroo clan can eat of the bandicoot. Each sees to the well-being of its own animal kinsmen so that others can eat and so that all life will remain in balance.

                                   * * * * *

"From Wakan Tanka there came a great unifying life force that flowed in and through all things--the flowers of the plains, blowing winds, rocks, trees, birds, animals--and was the same force that had been breathed into the first man. Thus all things were kindred and brought together by the same Great Mystery.... Kinship with all creatures of the earth, sky, and water was a real and active principle.... The animal had rights--the right of man's protection, the right to live, the right to multiply, the right to freedom, the right to man's indebtedness--and in recognition of these rights the Lakota never enslaved the animal, and spared all life that was not needed for food and clothing."

So wrote Luther Standing Bear in *Land of the Spotted Eagle* (1933).

                                   * * * * *

"All ethics so far evolved rest upon a single premise: that the individual is a member of a community of interdependent parts.... The land ethic simply enlarges the boundaries of the community to include soils, waters, plants, and animals, or collectively: the land.... In short, a land ethic changes the role of *Homo sapiens* from conqueror of the land-community to plain member and citizen of it. It implies respect for his fellow-members, and also respect for the community as such.... A system of conservation based solely on economic self-interest is hopelessly lopsided. It tends to ignore, and thus eventually to eliminate, many elements in the land community that lack commercial value, but that are (as far as we know) essential to its healthy functioning.... A land, ethic, then, reflects the existence of an ecological conscience, and this in turn reflects a conviction of individual responsibility for the health of the land. Health is the capacity of the land for self-renewal.   Conservation is our effort to understand and preserve that capacity."

So wrote the American naturalist Aldo Leopold in *A Sand County Almanac* (1966).

* * * * *

Words of Karora have been heard and sung. Images of Karora on churinga boards and on ground and body paintings have been viewed and worn. And you have danced with Karora and his Bandicoot Sons, and in the *Alcheringa.*

After the churinga boards are placed back in their cache, the designs on body and ground removed and the songs stored in memory, the short journey to camp is made. Each who had just participated is secure in the understanding that the wisdom and spirit of Karora is alive in the Dreamtime, and, as it is alive, so are you. The world is made.

* * * * *

From Walden Pond came two years of living "deliberately" in Nature. Henry David Thoreau (1817-1862) closely observed and recorded the intricate movements of squirrel and red maple, of clear air and ice, of soil and sunlight, all in their changing seasons. But in going out into Nature, the journey into his own soul had begun. Thoreau, like his friend Ralph Waldo Emerson (1803-1882), was an American Transcendentalist. The natural world of physical objects was a reflection of and given form by the universal spiritual truths of the transcendent reality. The overt beauty of the flower reflects its spiritual essence. "Nature is the symbol of the spirit...the world is emblematic," wrote

Emerson. It was then, through the soul and with the application of imagination, that humanity could escape its material forms and know of the spiritual truths. To go into Nature is to go into one's own soul, exploring its depths as the richness and animation of the tree and squirrel are explored.

"Nature is the incarnation of a thought, and turns to a thought again, as ice becomes water and gas. The world is mind precipitated, and the volatile essence is forever escaping again into the state of free thought." So wrote Emerson.

* * * * *

The man was diagnosed with diabetes. The physician put him on a strict diet and told him to come in regularly for insulin injections. It was the treatment.

But dieting is not an easy task in a society that emphasizes the social value of eating and food sharing. And who wants to take injections, especially when you know of a cure?

The man continued to come into the Indian Health Service Hospital for a checkup and to have his blood sugar levels monitored. But it was obvious to the physician that his patient was not losing any weight, and he knew the insulin injections were not being administered.

After several weeks, the physician realized that there was something quite remarkable going on with the condition of his patient. His blood sugar levels were approaching normal, and his diabetic sores had healed!

Curious, the physician began inquiring. It turns out that his patient had also become the patient of an *akbaalia*, "one who doctors," a Crow Indian medicine man. The *akbaalia* had given the diabetic his "brew" to take on a regular basis. The bitter-tasting drink is made from a particular plant that grows only at a certain location.

The physician met with the *akbaalia*, wanting to know more about the "brew" and if perhaps it could be administered by himself. The *akbaalia* told of the "brew" and listened to the request of the physician. But he informed the physician that he, the *akbaalia*, could not make such a decision allowing others to administer the medicine. That was a decision only the spirit fathers of the medicine can make. They are the true owners of the medicine. The human *akbaalia* is simply a caretaker of the "brew." In addition, the effectiveness of the "brew" was only partly the result of the physical properties of the plant. The real power of the "brew" comes from its *baaxpee*, its spiritual essence. It comes from the spirit world. And that is something the IHS physicians have never understood very well and certainly could not administer. The physician left with a better appreciation of his Crow counterpart, but without the "brew."

* * * * *

"Crazy Horse dreamed and went into the world where there is nothing but the spirits of all things. That is the real world that is behind this one, and everything we see here is something like a shadow from that world."

So spoke Black Elk (1862-1950), a Lakota holy man.

* * * * *

Behold! human beings living in an underground cave. They have been there since birth, their legs and necks chained to the wall. They can look only to the front, toward the wall opposite them. Above and behind them at a distance a fire burns bright. Between the cave opening and the fire various people pass by, carrying all sorts of things such as vessels and statues and even figures of animals carved of wood. The shadows of those passing by and what they carry are cast upon the cave wall. What is seen by the prisoners is their world, is their truth.

Some of the prisoners are released from their chains. Still in the cave, they look around and, at first, are blinded by the bright light and suffer sharp pains. They are unable to see the realities of what formerly were the source of the shadows. As they grow accustomed to the light, they realize the illusion of what they had seen and the real existence of what they now see. They see the carved images that were being carried by those passing by.

The prisoners are then reluctantly dragged up entirely out from the cave into the world of the sun. Again they are blinded and suffer much pain. But as they become accustomed to the

bright light, they begin to see. At first only the shadows of
things, then the reflections off the waters, and finally the things
themselves are seen. They see the animals that had been the
inspiration for the wood carvings. Then the moon and stars, and
finally the sun itself are seen by those who once only knew of
the shadows cast upon the walls of their cave. What had been
reality is now shown to be an illusion, and what was thought to
be an illusion is now shown to be reality. It is the ideas behind
the overt that are indeed the real. Out from the cave came the
prisoners into the light. The sun is seen!

One of the prisoners decides to go back into the cave and
free the others. At first he is blinded by the darkness, but then
grows accustomed to the lack of light. And then he realizes his
foolishness. If he should try to convince the prisoners that the
shadows are illusions, they would only argue that he is wrong,
blinded by the bright light. If he should try to bring them up out
of the cave, the prisoners would certainly kill him!

And so Plato (428-347 B.C.) told of the parable of the cave
in *Republic*, Book VII.

* * * * *

The following illustrations are the reverse sides of a churinga
board. The board is from the Aranda (an Australian Aborigine
people) and represents the Frog spirit, an expression of the
Alcheringa. The wood carving is 39 centimeters in length. On
the churinga, the three prominent sets of concentric circles are
the celebrated gum-tree at the sacred site near Hugh River. It is
out of these trees that the frog comes forth. On the first side
(top), the double concentric circles are the bodies of small frogs
having just emerged from the trees. The lines connecting them
are their limbs. On the reverse side (bottom), the three gum-trees
are again seen. The series of lines extending from them are their
roots. The smaller concentric circles are less important gum-trees
with their roots. The dots are the tracks of the frogs as they hop
about in the sand of the river bed.

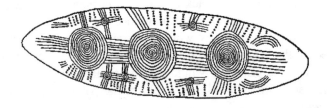

* * * * *

"Consider a tree and a man and an axe. We observe that the axe flies through the air and makes certain sorts of gashes in a pre-existing cut in the side of the tree...."

To understand this set of phenomena, or any set of phenomena, Gregory Bateson would have us understand the exchanges and flows of "ideas" and "information," or more precisely, the register of the "differences in" the component parts making up the entire phenomena. Following the German philosopher Immanuel Kant, an elementary unit of "information" is but the degree of difference registered within and between entities, a "*difference which makes a difference.*" In considering a tree and a man and an axe, we would be concerned with the "differences in" the cut in the face of the tree, the retina of the man, his central nervous system, his efferent neural messages, the behavior of his muscles, the velocity and edge of the axe head, the angle of the cut, the tenacity of the wood fibers, and again, the cut in the face of that tree. Each interaction involved a certain exchange of information, and depending on the nature of that information, what was exchanged is the observed result. For instance, the wood fiber and the edge of the axe were each the recipients of the information of the other. And the "difference in" the two, the information exchanged, even so slight, will alter the character of the cut and thus the entire phenomenon. In turn, each and every interaction and exchange forms an integral part of a continuous and total circuit of information flows which intersects, transcends and abrogates the specific boundaries of any given component. If you want to explain or understand anything, you must comprehend the completed circuit of information flows.

This is an "elementary cybernetic thought," with its "transform of differences traveling in a circuit," and is characterized as a "total information-processing, trial-and-error completing unit." In turn, it is a part of an all-inclusive "hierarchy of subsystem" networks. This entire cybernetic system is synonymous with "Mind," a mental system. It can be expressed simply, in the messages exchanged between an axe head and the wood fibers. It can certainly be identified in the operations of your own mind. And most importantly, Mind is "immanent in the large biological system--the ecosystem."

We have generally come to know an ecology in terms of its "bioenergetics--the economics of energy and materials within a coral reef, a redwood forest, or a city." But an ecology has another face, that of "an economics of information, of entropy, negentropy, etc.," a cybernetic ecology. It is a system not so readily identifiable. For its properties are not discrete, concrete units, that which we are accustomed to viewing. In fact, neither ecosystem coincides with the other, as each is bounded differently. In bioenergetics, the units are bounded at the cell membrane--the skin of a plant or an animal--or "units composed of sets of conspecific individuals." It is within these boundaries that we can measure the "addictive-subtractive budget of energy for the given unit." By contrast, informational ecology focuses on the budgeting of messages along pathways and of their probabilities. "The resulting budgets are fractionating," rather than addictive-subtractive; while the boundaries must "enclose the relevant pathways," transcending the boundaries of the conspecific units.

"Moreover, the very meaning of 'survival' becomes different when we stop talking about the survival of something bounded by the skin and start to think of the survival of the system of ideas in circuit. The contents of the skin are randomized at death and the pathways within the skin are randomized. But the ideas, under further transformation, may go on out in the world in books or works of art. Socrates as a bioenergetic individual is dead. But much of him still lives as a component in the contemporary ecology of ideas....

The cybernetic epistemology which I have offered you would suggest a new approach. The individual mind is immanent but not only in the body. It is immanent also in pathways and messages outside the body; and there is a larger Mind of which the individual mind is only a subsystem. This larger Mind is comparable to God and is perhaps what some people mean by 'God,' but it is still immanent in the total interconnected social system and planetary ecology....

If you put God outside and set him vis-a-vis his creation and if you have the idea that you are created in his image, you will logically and naturally see yourself as outside and against the things around you. And as you arrogate all mind to yourself, you will see the world around you as mindless and therefore not entitled to moral or ethical consideration. The environment will seem to be yours to exploit. Your survival unit will be you and your folks or conspecifics against the environment of the social units, other races and the brutes and vegetables.

If this is your estimate of your relation to nature *and you have an advanced technology*, your likelihood of survival will be that of a snowball in hell. You will die either of the toxic by-products of your own hate, or, simply, of overpopulation and overgrazing. The raw materials of the world are finite....

It is the attempt to *separate* intellect from emotion that is monstrous, and I suggest that it is equally monstrous--and dangerous--to attempt to separate the external mind from the internal. Or to separate mind from body....

The creature that wins against its environment destroys itself."

So wrote the anthropologist Gregory Bateson (1904-1980) in *Steps to an Ecology of Mind* (1972).

* * * * *

"We did not think of the great open plains, the beautiful rolling hills, the winding streams with tangled growth, as 'wild.' Only to the white man was nature a 'wilderness' and only to him was the land 'infested' with 'wild' animals and 'savage' people. To us it was tame. Earth was bountiful and we were surrounded with the blessings of the Great Mystery. Not until the hairy man from the east came and with brutal frenzy heaped injustices upon us and the families we loved was it 'wild' for us. When the very animals of the forest began fleeing from his approach, then it was that for us the 'Wild West' began."

So wrote Luther Standing Bear in *Land of the Spotted Eagle* (1933).

* * * * *

"History means disrespect for the ancestors."

So echoed the voice of the Lakota leader, Sitting Bull (1831-1890).

* * * * *

The shape of the perfectly formed petals, the color of unmatched red, the image of beauty that bursts forth through the grasses: all is God-inspired. You stand there, without a word exchanged. But in the silence you've heard, oh so clearly.

After a moment, or was it longer? a glance down, a glance to the sky, and with hand raised and voice, you give "thanks," and continue on through the trees.

The Lesson[17]

The school bell had just rung, and you and the other students make your way, rather hurriedly, to the desks. With the exception of a few in the back row who choose to continue their conversation, all eyes and ears focus front. Notebooks are opened to white sheets of paper. Pencils are ready. The teacher enters the classroom and the lesson begins. Lecture is augmented by demonstration. On the blackboard, the key concepts and their symbols are written down; a flow chart is sketched out. On the front desk, the panel of lights glow and electrical circuits flow with an unseen but measurable energy. Observations are made and scientific principles lead to conclusions. And the school bell rings again.

*   *   *   *   *

Francis Bacon (1561-1623), influential in the development of the scientific revolution, maintained that only a very particular sort of knowledge is worthy of pursuing. That knowledge is technological knowledge, the knowledge of how something works. Such knowledge is less the knowledge of why something works. The distinction between applied and formal science was made. It is the knowledge that has direct application and utility for man. Born is the doctrine that what is valued and good is that which is useful to man--utilitarianism. And with this knowledge, man is given power over nature; nature will do his bidding. Knowledge is power. Because it is for man, it should be knowledge made public and shared. In 1620, Bacon published his *Novum Organum* that set out his approach to inquiry and knowledge. To acquire this technological knowledge, Bacon was among the first to propose an inductive method based on observation.

---

[17]For additional background, see Hall 1983, Matthews 1989 and Nasr 1982.

* * * * *

The English philosopher, John Locke (1632-1704), stated, in *Essay concerning Human Understanding*, that the mind is as a "white paper, void of all characters, without ideas," like an "empty cabinet," as yet unfurnished. The mind is *tabula rasa*, a blank slate. The material to furnish the cabinet is the knowledge that comes from experience. For Locke, all knowledge is founded on observation, the senses. And so is founded the empirical method, i.e., "relating to experience." Knowledge is the precise correspondence between what is observed by the human senses and what exists in the natural world.

The world Locke is referring to is the natural world of physics, chemistry, biology, psychology and sociology. It is a world that exists independent of the mind, with its own structures and governed by its own processes, all of which can be discovered through rigorous observation.

The empiricist begins with observations of the natural world. These observations must be controlled, objective, verifiable and replicative. Subjectivity must be kept out. The observations are based on those senses that can be controlled and objective, i.e., sight, sound, smell, touch and taste. An example of an empirical observation would be--the walls of Jericho are 2.7 meters thick, 3.2 meters high and seven hundred meters in circumference.

The empiricist then forms a hypothesis that attempts to account for the observations. The process is called induction, i.e., reasoning from a limited number of observations to a conclusion or hypothesis. For example, the walls of Jericho are built to keep something out and to keep something safely within them.

From the hypothesis, testing begins. Deliberate, systematic experimentation and extensive observation now occur to discover if the hypothesis is indeed correct or needing revision. The hypothesis is tested. The attempt is to verify what was originally observed. Replication is the criteria for verification. At Jericho, the empiricist might observe the types of objects kept within the walls, distinct from those found outside the walls. What is observed are the trappings of a domesticated people within the walls: quantities of stored food stuffs, valuable trade items, finely crafted tools. All valuable objects. Further observation shows that these objects are not to be found among those who lived outside the walls of Jericho. This would lead the empiricist to conclude that the walls are indeed built to keep something out and to keep something safely within.

If a reasonable verification results, the empiricist then ventures a prediction of what will be discovered under similar natural circumstances. When walls similar to those at Jericho are found, they are likely built to keep something out and to keep something safely within. The strength and legitimacy of the empirical method is its ability to predict what occurs in the natural world.

* * * * *

The French philosopher, Rene Descartes (1596-1650), approached knowledge from quite a different stance than did John Locke. For Descartes, man has ultimate knowledge of his own existence because he is a thinking being--*cogito ergo sum*-- "I think, therefore I am." Thus the foundations of knowledge consist of a set of first, "self-evident" principles, *a priori principles*. The mind is not an empty cabinet but is filled with universal, though not readily known, principles.

Access to these first principles is not based on "the fluctuating testimony of the senses" nor on the "blundering constructions of imagination." Descartes distrusted sensory evidence as much as he avoided undisciplined imagination. The first principles are those based on "the conception which an unclouded and attentive mind gives." It is conception "wholly freed from doubt," principles derived from clear and logical thought. From these first principles, other truths can be deduced by a rigorous application of logical rules and axioms.

Knowledge is not so much what corresponds to experience but what has coherency within and among the principles and their deduced statements. And so the rational method is born. Descartes published his approach to knowledge in 1637, in

Discourse on Method.

The rationalist begins with a set of assumptions that are hypothetically true. For instance, Jericho is a community settled by people. The walls of Jericho are defensive walls. Defense is an activity for defending something. All of these assumptions need not be verified by observation, need not exist in fact. They need only be hypothetically correct. Implicit from these assumptions, a deduction can now be made logically. The people of Jericho have something to defend. Mathematically-rigorous formulas are applied in order to arrive at the deductions. The strength and legitimacy of the rational method is its ability to objectively think about the natural world and deduce statements of truth about that world.

* * * * *

"Examining attentively what I was, and seeing that I could pretend that I had no body and that there was no world or place that I was in, but that I could not for all that pretend that I did not exist, and that on the contrary, from the very fact that I thought of doubting the truth of other things, it followed very evidently and very certainly that I existed: while on the other hand, if I had only ceased to think, although the rest of what I had ever imagined had been true, I would have had no reason to believe that I existed; I thereby concluded that I was a substance of which the whole essence or nature consists in thinking, and which, in order to exist, needs no place and depends upon no material thing; so that this I, that is to say mind, by which I am what I am, is entirely distinct from the body, and even that is easier to know than the body, and moreover, that even if the body were not, it would not cease to be all that it is." (*Discourse on Method*, 54)

Rene Descartes made another important contribution. Descartes reasoned that if the mind is capable of clear, objective thinking, then it cannot ultimately be reducible to the influences of the material world. "Mind" and "matter" are the basic constituents of the universe. The defining characteristic of "matter" is extension and movement, i.e., the possession of dimension such as time or space. The defining characteristic of "mind" is thought, i.e., the activity of thinking. Regardless of the way "matter" is extended, e.g., straight or curved, it must be extended. Regardless of the way "mind" thinks, e.g., abstracting or imagining, it must think. Each is absolutely different from the other, requiring nothing but itself to exist. Neither has the properties of the other nor is reducible to the other, yet all in the universe is reducible to one or the other, to "mind" or "matter."

Cartesian Dualism affirms that the natural world of matter is independent of the mind, and the mind is independent of the natural world. Objectivity is possible. The world of the "other" and of man himself have become objects, for study.

* * * * *

Long after the lecture is forgotten, the knowledge it conveyed can still be applied to virtually every aspect of your life. Empiricism and rationalism ushered forth a powerful methodology for harnessing the natural resources of the world. Electricity is at work for you and your fellow students, at a flick of a switch.

The Quest[18]

You're among those gathered around the kitchen table, young in the ways of your people. Another carries with him the wisdom of the stories. The evening meal is finished, the table cleared and the story begins.

* * * * *

There's a young boy...
It's early evening,
      he's just finished with his meal.

---

[18]The story text is from the contemporary Crow people of Montana. The story of Burnt Face expresses a common literary motif found throughout North American Indian oral literature. For additional ethnographic background, see Brown 1953, Frey 1987, Furst and Furst 1982, Gill 1982, Lowie 1918 and Nabokov and Easton 1989.

There he goes..
That boy is running through camp,
>> between lodges,
>>>> chasing someone?...
It's his sister!..
There they go,
>> around that lodge,
>>>> over there.
Faster he goes,
>> not very careful where he plants his feet...
He's just about to catch up with her.
He reaches out to grab her.
He falls,
>> falls right into a fire pit....
His face lands,
>> where the coals of a fire still glow bright red.
All of the right side of the face is badly burnt!..
Cries of pain are heard throughout the camp.
An old man comes running toward the boy.
He gathers up the soft leaves of Prairie-dog-tail,
>> which grows here,...
>>>> there..
He places the leaves in his mouth,
>> chews on them..
Standing over the boy,
>> the old man very carefully lays the poultice of leaves
>> on the face.
The burnt face can now heal,
>> yet tears still flow from the eyes of that young boy..
Throughout the night,
>> the old man,.
>>>> and the parents care for the boy,
>>>>>> a boy who had run so carelessly
>>>>>> through camp..
By morning the pain is gone,
>> a face bad to look at remains...

It's a terrible scar the boy must now live with...
Some time passes....
The young boy comes out from his parent's lodge.
Others,
      his sisters,
          his brothers,
             his friends,
                gather around to see him..
What they see is bad to look at.
They poke fun at the boy,.
      tease him...
"Burnt Face,
      hey,
          Burnt Face!" they say...
His eyes look to the ground,
      fill with tears...
That boy returns to the warmth of his parent's lodge..
Some time passes....
It's evening,
      a great dance is taking place.
All are in their finest beaded buckskins,
      they have their faces painted in bright colors,
         reds,
            yellows,
              blues,
                black,
                  white..

Good song is heard,
      everyone is dancing..
Here comes the boy they call Burnt Face..
His friends gather around to see.
What they see,
      through the bright colored paint,
         is a face,...
            bad to look at.

They tease,
        they poke fun at the young boy.
"Burnt Face," they say..
His eyes look to the ground,
        fill with tears....
Sometime ago,
        he'd been careless,
                fell into a fire pit.
All of the right side of his face is burnt,
        he's bad to look at...
Burnt Face goes back into his parent's lodge.
Seldom does he come out..
Some time passes....
"Mother,
        make me four pairs of moccasins," he says.
She knows what her son must do,
        she does not want to make the moccasins..
A sweat bath is taken.
In the heat,
        prayers are given.
The boy is cleaned from the inside out...
A pair of the deer-skin moccasins are put on.
Dried meat is packed into the other moccasins..
He holds his father's finely carved pipe,
        his beaded pipe bag,
                and Burnt Face leaves his parent's lodge.
He heads for the great mountains to the south.
You know,
        all true wisdom is to be found far from the dwellings
        of men,
                in the great solitudes.....
It'll be a long journey,.
        Burnt Face is alone.
A little meat is eaten,
        cool water from the stream that runs close by is taken..

After awhile,
>holes are worn in the soles of his moccasins,
>>another pair is put on..

Farther he goes into the hill country.
Holes again come to his moccasins,
>another pair are put on..

The forest is thick with tall trees..
Burnt Face continues toward the high mountains..
A little more meat is eaten.
Holes come,
>another pair of moccasins are put on.

The trees are gone,...
>rock,
>>wind everywhere...

Burnt Face goes higher into the mountains.
The dried meat is gone,
>holes are worn in the soles of the fourth pair of
>moccasins..

Burnt Face is barefoot,.
>he continues where there is snow.

It is mid-summer,
>the mountains here contain the cold of snow.

On a high ridge,
>where the Sun's rise,
>>where the Sun's set can clearly be seen,
>>>Burnt Face rests..

It's a good place...
The pipe is filled with willow bark,
>with bearberry leaf,
>>with kinnikinick,.
>>>the pipe is lit....

Burnt Face begins his prayer.
      "Spirit people,.
            Bird people,.
                   Animal people,.
                          take pity on me..
      My face is bad to look at...
      I hate part of myself.
      Sometime ago I was careless,
            fell into a fire pit.
      The right side of my face is scarred,
            they call me 'Burnt Face.'".....
And he looks to the ground..
On this high ridge,
      he takes no water,.
            no food....
He gives up these things so that his prayers can be heard,
      that someone will come,
            that someone will take pity on him......
With each rise of the Sun,
      with each setting of the Sun,
            the pipe is filled with kinnikinick,
                with fire.
Prayer is offered.
As the smoke rises,
      so too do the words of the prayer..
Under the Sun's watch,
      Burnt Face spends his days moving stones.
This stone here,...
      that stone are selected,.
            and carried to the ridge..
There's a good stone..
A great circle is formed,
      rows of stone out from a center,
            some eighty paces across.
It's a gift to the Sun....

You know,
      it can still be seen today,
           high in the Bighorn Mountains.
They call it a Medicine Wheel..
                  * * * * *

Big Horn Medicine Wheel

    The way of the world is a great circle. It has no beginning, nor an end, for time is as a circle, always repeating itself. The life of any four-legged or two-legged is as a circle, from birth, to maturity, to old age, and back to where one came. The sun, the moon, the stars and the earth are as circles and move in circles as well. The great winds move in circles, move around the stones, trees and flowers that are all rounded as the circle. The birds make their nests as circles and their young are born out of the circles of eggs.

This we all see with the circles of our eyes and come to know in our hearts. This we live by. Our lodges were once round as the nests of birds; now we are reminded of this when we set up our tepees each August at Crow Fair. Throughout our land our ancestors built great circles of rock, which we now call medicine wheels. At our pow wows at New Year's and during Crow Fair we dance the round dance. We give prayer and clean ourselves from the inside out each time we enter the circle of our sweat lodges. When the medicine bundles are opened, we sit in a prayer circle and watch the smoke circle from our cigarettes, carrying our prayers with it. Each summer, when we build and give of ourselves within the circle of our Sun Dance lodge, we are reminded of the great circle of life and of the world.

Our lives and the lives of all the peoples make up a "great wagon wheel." Though the non-Indian came to this land on them, we've always had the "wheel." Ours can be seen in the rock medicine wheels and in the Sun Dance lodges. Each spoke of the great wheel is as a particular religion, a particular people-- the Sun Dance, the Christian, the Moslem, the Hindu, the Buddhist, the Indian, the non-Indian, the two-leggeds, the four-leggeds, the wingeds. Each is unique, with its own language and traditions. But all are of equal worth; all are of the same length. To shorten or even remove one of the spokes would only cause the wheel to wobble and fall. All are needed. Nevertheless, all the spokes are linked to the same hub, the same God. Though each of us may address it differently, each with our own way of praying, it is the same God, uniting all the peoples. To live is to live in the circle, as a part of the great wheel.

* * * * *

"One should pay attention to even the smallest crawling creature, for these too may have a valuable lesson to teach us, and even the smallest ant may wish to communicate with a man."

So Black Elk spoke.

* * * * *

The days pass,
     one,
          two,
               three..
Burnt Face grows weaker..
Prayers continue to be offered,
     stones are moved....
It's the morning of the fourth day..
Burnt Face is looking east,
     out over the trees that lie below the high ridge.
He looks among the trees,
     something catches his eyes.
Something is moving through the trees!...
The trees bend this way,
     then that..
It's moving slowly toward the ridge..
It's a,...
     a whirlwind,
          a strong wind.
That's what it is...
The trees begin to bend so far over that they break!
They're like twigs,
     snapping at the power of the whirlwind.
Closer it comes..
Burnt Face feels the strength of the wind.
He leans into it,
     and his long black braids are blown back from his
     face.
He thinks that it would be wise to run fast from this great
wind.
Burnt Face remembers what his grandfather says,
     "The gifts often come when you least expect them."...
The pipe is in hand.
Burnt Face holds his ground.

The whirlwind is just about to blow Burnt Face off the ridge,
      into the valley below,.
           when it stops...
The wind is gone....
Where the wind had been there now stands,.
      a great Eagle...

* * * * *

While asleep, an *aassahkee*, a clan uncle has a dream, a vision of an event that is yet to occur. In his dream he sees his clan nephew walking up to an eagle and pulling, from its twelve tail feathers, the two center feathers, the evenly matched ones. This he sees clearly in a dream.

The next day, he shares the dream with another elder of the tribe, but not with the young man seen in the dream.

Several weeks pass. The young man of the dream is driving back to the reservation from Billings on the Interstate. Something catches his eye, and curious, he pulls over onto the shoulder of the highway. A rock outcropping now shields what caught his eye, so he takes a walk. What he finds is an eagle. It must be injured, for it does not attempt to fly off as he approaches. The eagle just looks at him. He doesn't know why, but as he stands over the bird, he reaches down and pulls the evenly-matched pair of the twelve tail feathers from the eagle! The eagle continues to look on. Once the feathers are in hand, the bird takes to the sky and flies off to the east.

The young man doesn't know what to make of all this. So he takes the feathers and the story to an elder and tells what had just occurred. And the old man tells him of the dream his clan uncle had some time before and that these feathers were meant to be his. They were a gift from the Eagle to the young man. The feathers were blessed in the smoke of sweet grass and given prayers. They are now used by the young man when he dances in the Sun Dance. The Eagle is close by.

* * * * *

"Why are you crying,
      my son?" the Eagle says.

"Because I hate part of myself,
          I'm bad to look at.
          Sometime ago I was careless,
                    fell into a fire pit.
          All of the right side of my face is badly burnt,
                    they call me 'Burnt Face,'" he says.
"If you'll help me,
          my family,
                    we'll help you," he says.
Burnt Face thinks that's a good idea...
Burnt Face gets on the back of the huge Eagle,
          holds on tight.
It's a huge bird...
The boy feels light,
          they are among the clouds,
                    flying to a land far to the south..
When he looks down,
          everything is so small,
                    he gets a little dizzy...
You know,
          Burnt Face hadn't done much flying!...
So he keeps his eyes tightly closed,
          not wanting to look down,
                    hoping the Eagle will soon land...
Some time passes....
The great Eagle begins to fly low,
          just over the tops of the trees.
It's a land strange,
          unknown to Burnt Face..
Just ahead is a clearing filled with tall grasses.
A camp is to one side.
It's the camp of the Eagle,.
          his family..
The journey has come to an end,
          Burnt Face feels heavy again,
                    glad to plant his feet on the ground again...

Burnt Face is greeted by two small Eagles,
          children of the Bird.
"Why are you crying,
          my brother," they say.
"Because I hate part of myself.
          I'm bad to look at.
          Sometime ago I was careless,
                    fell into a fire pit.
          All of the right side of my face was burnt.
          They call me,
                    'Burnt Face,'" he says.
"Over the ridge there,
          there's a fast moving river.
          In that river,
                    lives the Long Otter..
          He sneaks about in the brush,
                    tries to take my children.
          We're not safe....
          You must help," he says..
It's a huge otter,...
          very dangerous..
Burnt Face offers to do what he can to help.
He's just a small boy,
          and it's the Long Otter!....
Burnt Face heads for the river.
Along the way he picks up four rocks,
          like those used in a sweat lodge ceremony,
                    he brings them along..
At the river's bank,
          dried driftwood is gathered.
He piles it high...
A fire is lit.
The four stones are placed on top.
Soon the rock is filled with fire.
Each stone glows bright red...

A little more wood is gathered,
            the fire is kept alive..
Burnt Face waits..
Some time passes.....
A fog moves off the river's waters,
            covers the day with darkness!..
A stillness is everywhere.
The birds can no longer be heard......
The fog is gone.
It is as it was.
The birds are heard,
            the sun shine upon the waters,
                        the trees.
It's all very strange....
The fog again clouds the day into night,
            not a sound can be heard..
The wind had rustled through the leaves of the trees.
Now all is still....
The fog is gone.
It's day again...
The fog comes again,
            the light,
                        the sounds of day are gone.
The waters could be heard splashing up against the river's
rocks.
Now it's quiet....
As fast as it came,
            the fog is gone.
The Sun is bright in the sky...
The fog moves over the land again,
            bringing a darkness,
                        a stillness with it....
The day becomes a night,
            nothing can be seen,
                        nothing can be heard.....
Burnt Face waits....

All is still.....
Something is heard in the fog!
It's very faint...
It gets louder,....
          louder....
Thump,.
          thump,.
                    thump...
Louder it gets..
Right in front of Burnt Face,
          the outstretched jaws of the Long Otter....
Shining in the darkness,
          the sharp teeth of the huge beast.
Just like that,
          Burnt Face throws one,
                    two,
                              then a third.
Then the fourth,
          red hot rock goes into the mouth that seeks something
          else.
The rocks burn the stomach,.
          steam,
                    smoke bellows from the mouth.
The Long Otter rolls this way,
          then that,
                    back into the waters of the river.
The Long Otter swims off,.
          never to be seen again...
The Sun returns,
          bright,
                    warm..
The birds sing a glorious song..
The great Eagle is there.
"Look into the waters of the river there," he says.
Burnt Face looks down...
Tears fall into that which he sees.

What Burnt Face sees he had hated.
He no longer has hate.
What had brought him so much pain is now gone.
The tears are of..joy...
The Eagle pulls from its tail one of its feathers,
        places it in the hand of Burnt Face.
"When you are in need call upon me with this feather,
        I will stand at your side," he says.
The Eagle is as a father to Burnt Face....
Burnt Face journeys north,
        back to his family,.
                this time he stays on the ground..
He'd had enough flying...
He enters camp.
His parents,
        sisters,
                brothers,
                        all of the camp gather around Burnt
                        Face..
None poke fun at him.
None tease him.
Tears fill the eyes of many.
What they see is a young man,
        strong,
                true,
                        a man who will become a great leader
                        among his people.....
It's said that Burnt Face lived to such a great age,
        that he was so old that when he moved about,.
                his skin would tear...
That's old!...

                        * * * * *

    "Everything was possessed of personality, only differing with us in form. Knowledge was inherent in all things. The world was a library and its books were the stones, leaves, grass, brooks, and the birds and animals that shared, alike with us, the storms and blessings of earth. We learned to do what only the student of nature ever learns and that was to feel beauty."

So wrote Luther Standing Bear in *Land of the Spotted Eagle* (1933).

* * * * *

Later that summer, a vow is made to give of yourself. In the heat and steam of the sweat lodge, words of prayer are spoken. When you leave the canvas-covered lodge you're cleaned "from the inside out."   Alone, you make your way to the high mountains.   All true wisdom is to be found far from the dwellings of men. There you offer yourself up, going without food and water. You offer up sincerity, *diakaashe*, "really doing it." With the rising and setting of the sun, cigarettes are lit and prayers offered. In the smoke the words go forth. An offering is given. And you listen, listen with your "heart."

On the third day a visitor arrives. It's one of the *Awakkule*, the Little People, who live in the mountains and reveal themselves only when a special gift is to be given. A vision is received that will guide you your entire life. The *Awakkule* have adopted you as their child.

Three Hots and a Cot[19]

You have a good job and you've worked hard. For several years now, the savings account had grown, but oh so slowly. Much has been sacrificed: that trip to Mexico, a second car, and all the endless little things. You've even held off starting a family. Each month you've paid the rent and there's been nothing to show for it. But now a down payment could be made on what had only been dreamt of for so long. Though the property taxes will be high, it'll be a nice neighborhood, with stores close by. It'll be yours!

---

[19]For additional background, see Jesser 1975 and Sahlins 1976.

* * * * *

"Early to bed, and early to rise, makes a man healthy, wealthy, and wise."

"God helps them that help themselves."

"Lost time is never found again."

"Plough deep while sluggards sleep, and you shall have corn to sell and keep, says Poor Dick."

"He that lives upon hope will die fasting."

"There are no gains without pains."

"If you would be wealthy, think of saving as well as of getting."

So wrote Benjamin Franklin (1706-1790) in *Poor Richard's Almanac* (1733-1758).

* * * * *

It was Adam Smith (1723-1790), the Scottish political philosopher and economist, who laid out the fundamental principles of laissez-faire capitalism in his *An Inquiry into the Nature and Causes of the Wealth of Nations*, published in 1776. Primary among these principles is his clarification of a basic human motivation. According to Smith, man is, by nature, acquisitive. People are driven by the desire to accumulate material wealth. And it is a demand that is never satisfied. It is a drive innate within all of humanity, a drive to maximize one's own gains and to minimize one's own losses; it is the drive for self-interest. In the ebbs and flows of the supply and demand market-place, this desire fuels the system and is measured in terms of profit. As such, capitalism is predicated on an ever-expanding economy; it is predicated on growth. Without this elementary human condition, capitalism would cease and collapse.[20]

* * * * *

"A penny saved is a penny earned."

---

[20]Capitalism had not manifested itself as a significant economic system prior to the European Renaissance. It flourished after the Renaissance (ca. 1600-present).

* * * * *

"Individualism is a word recently coined to express a new idea."

"Individualism is a calm and considered feeling which disposes each citizen to isolate himself from the mass of his fellows and withdraw into a circle of family and friends; with this little society formed to his taste, he gladly leaves the greater society to look after itself."

"There are more and more people who, though neither rich nor powerful enough to have much hold over others, have gained or kept enough wealth and enough understanding to look after their own needs. Such folk owe no man anything and hardly expect anything from anybody. They form the habit of thinking of themselves in isolation and imagine that their whole destiny is in their hands."

"Each man is forever thrown back on himself alone, and there is danger that he may be shut up in the solitude of his own heart," forgetting his ancestors, his descendants and isolating himself from his contemporaries.

"It is odd to watch with what feverish ardor Americans pursue prosperity, ever tormented by the shadowy suspicion that they may not have chosen the shortest route to get it. They cleave to the things of this world as if assured that they will never die, and yet rush to snatch any that come within their reach, as if they expected to stop living before they relished them. Death steps in, in the end, and stops them, before they have grown tired of this futile pursuit of that complete felicity which always escapes them."

So wrote the French social philosopher, Alex de Tocqueville, in *Democracy in America*. Tocqueville traveled throughout America of the 1830s, observing the emerging character of its people.

* * * * *

"Rugged individualism."

* * * * *

The English philosopher Herbert Spencer (1820-1903) added

Stories: The Texts

still another clarification of human motivation.   Borrowing loosely from the model of biological evolution as developed by Charles Darwin (1809-1882), Spencer applied an evolutionary model to human social institutions. Through time, human society evolves into more advanced states.   Progress is endemic to human institutions and is inevitable. The mechanism for this advancement is what Spencer called "survival of the fittest." Some individuals in society and some societies among various societies are better endowed than others to adapt to the rigors of competition.   They have a natural right to initiate, direct and benefit from societal institutions. Progress depends upon their initiatives. The human condition is a competitive condition. And a competitive individual is a strong and successful individual.

* * * * *

"Be the best you can be."

* * * * *

Karl Marx (1818-1883), the German political philosopher and economist, also advocated a doctrine of inevitable progress; but, a progress that would lead to a classless society. The mechanism driving this progress is dialectical materialism. Following Georg Wilhelm Friedrich Hegel (1770-1831), Marx maintained that history is a struggle between opposing societal forces, i.e., a thesis and an antithesis. Out of this dynamic, a new synthesis emerges. Unlike Hegel, Marx held that primary in this struggle are the material conditions that prevail in society. Marx reversed Hegel's position which held that consciousness defined the praxis. For Marx, the "modes of production," how people make a living, determines the entire societal infrastructure. What drives humans are their material needs. The structures of the family, the religious institutions and the belief systems of a people are molded by their "modes of production."   Demonstration of dialectical materialism is found in the feudal society of the Middle Ages. Nobility and clergy formed the thesis, while a growing trade-oriented middle class, the bourgeoisie, formed as an antithesis in this class struggle. Following the French and American revolutions, a synthesis emerged, forming the capitalist class. The new class, in turn, oppressed the workers, the proletariat, which represents the new antithesis. The struggle continues, with economics driving the entire system.

* * * * *

One of the most influential theories on the development of a healthy personality was that proposed by the American humanistic psychologist Abraham Maslow (1908-1970). The premise of Maslow's theory of human motivation is what he called a "hierarchy of needs." There are five levels of human achievement, each of which must be satisfied before the next can be attempted. The first level comprises the basic physiological needs, such as food, clothing and shelter. The second level revolves around safety and security needs. Love and belonging needs are expressed at the third level. The fourth level focuses on the needs of self-esteem. And the final level, the fifth level, comprises what Maslow calls "self-actualization." This level focuses on being well adjusted to one's entire situation and reality. It is here where spiritual gratification and insight into truth are obtained. Because of the ascending and progressive requirements of these levels, few people ever reach self-actualization; and those who do are in a continual effort to maintain that state. Basic survival, the praxis needs, must first be satisfied before the higher levels of consciousness can be achieved.

* * * * *

Sticks and stones can break my bones, but names can never hurt me.

* * * * *

It's *Isaahkawuattee*,
        Old Man Coyote...[21]

---

[21]The story text is from the oral literature of the Crow people. The character of the trickster, who may win but usually losses in his games of artful deception, duped by his own trickery, is a prevalent literary motif found throughout all of Indian oral literature. For additional background, see Frey 1995, Lowie 1918 and Thompson 1929.

He's going about very hungry,
      in search of food.
He comes upon *Shiilape*,
      Little Fox,
           who's running across an iced lake!..
Tied to his tail is a small bell.
He runs.
The bell strikes the ice,
      creates little pockets of warm,
          juicy tallow...
It steams in the cold of the day..
Little Fox retraces his steps,
      picks the tallow out,
         eats it...
It goes down so nicely...
Old Man Coyote watches.
He wants that bell..
"Little Fox,
      will you part with your bell?
      I want your bell," he says..
"I need this bell,
      older brother.
      I depend on it for my food," he says..
"Give me your bell,
      younger brother....
      I'll give you,...
         my dart...
      Let's make an exchange," he says.
It's a beautiful dart,
      famous for it's accuracy.
Little Fox thinks it over,..
      it is a great dart...
"I'll trade with you,
      older brother," he says.
Old Man Coyote hands over his dart to Little Fox,
      as Little Fox gives Old Man Coyote the bell.

"Younger brother,
        let me hold my dart,
                one last time," he says...
He'd been so attached to it....
Little Fox hands over the dart.
With the bell in one hand,.
        with the dart in the other,.
                Old Man Coyote,...
                        quick turns around,
                                runs off fast.
Over that hill he goes...
"Do not use the bell more than four times on any one day," he
says.
Old Man Coyote is not interested in listening.
He has his bell,
        he has his dart.
He's quite the fellow....
Old Man Coyote is hungry,
        knows what he can do.
He ties the bell to a blanket.
He runs over an iced pond,
        the bell striking here,...
                there,
                        creating pockets of warm,
                                juicy tallow.
He retraces his steps,
        picks out the meal.
It goes down nicely,
        warming the inners of Old Man Coyote....
Old Man Coyote gets hungry again,
        he comes to an iced river..
Over it he runs,
        picks the warm tallow from the ice.
It's a great meal....
Some time passes...
Old Man Coyote is hungry again.

He always has a big appetite...
He runs across an iced lake,
          fast as he can.
The bell strikes here,..
          there,..
                    here,..
                              there...
He goes fast,
          slipping a little,
                    regaining his balance...
It's a wonderful feast,
          tallow smeared all over Old Man Coyote's whiskers....
The day is late,
          Old Man Coyote is again hungry..
He runs across an iced lake,
          the bell striking here,..
                    there..
He retraces his steps,
          he has a fine meal....
It isn't quite enough.
He's got his bell..
Old Man Coyote continues running across that lake,
          faster,
                    all around,
                              the bell striking here,.
                                        there..
Faster he goes.
Then it happens..
Old Man Coyote slips,...
          falls hard to the ice,
                    his bottom stuck to the ice,.
                              froze to it..
He can't move....
Prairie Chicken comes along.

"Older brother,
        what are you doing there,
                sitting on the ice?
        It must be awfully cold," he says....
Old Man Coyote is quick.
"I'm waiting for,...
        the dance we're going to have here,...
                we'll have a great feast right here...
        I need you to go out,
                fill your pouches with lots of raspberries.
        There will be a lot of us," he says...
Prairie Chicken goes out,
        gathers the raspberries...
Beaver comes along.
"Older brother,
        what are you doing there?
        It must be cold," he says...
"Younger brother,
        I need your help.
        We're going to have a wonderful dance here,
                a feast that follows.
        Go out,
                cut with your teeth two stout willow sticks.
                        big ones...
        I need drum sticks for the dance," he says..
So Beaver goes out,
        he brings in the two stout sticks...
Magpie comes along.
"Older brother,
        what are you doing sitting there on the ice.
        It must be pretty cold," he says...

"Younger brother,
        go out,
                announce with your great voice.
        Tell the animals that there will be a dance here,
                a great feast to follow.
        Call in the Jackrabbit,
                Prairie-dog,
                        Deer,
                                Elk.
        Call in Cottontail,
                call in Beaver.
        Don't call in,
                Skunk though," he says...
Magpie goes out,
        calls in all the animals Old Man Coyote wants..
Beaver is there,
        Jackrabbit,
                Deer,
                        Cottontail,
                                Elk,
                                        Prairie-dog is there...
"Younger brothers,
        let's have a fine dance,
                let's have a great feast to follow..
        Let me introduce to you a new dance step..
        I'll sing a good song,
                at the height of the song,
        I want you to close your eyes,...
                dance under my bottom," he says...
Now the animals have never heard of such a dance step.
They're willing to try it,
        at least once..
So Old Man Coyote starts in,
        beating on the ice,
                singing his song..
It's a fine song...

At the height of the song,
>   the animals close their eyes,
>>   dance under Old Man Coyote's,...
>>>   bottom....

He's freed..
And Old Man Coyote goes about,...
>   hitting the animals over the head..,
>   Jackrabbit,
>>   Prairie-dog,
>>>   Deer,

>>>>   Beaver,

>>>>>   Elk,

>>>>>>   Cottontail...

Old Man Coyote has a great feast....

* * * * *

"Wilderness--Land of No Use." (bumper sticker, anonymous)

* * * * *

"Wilderness is the raw material out of which man has hammered the artifact called civilization.... The rich diversity of the world's cultures reflect a corresponding diversity in the wilds that gave them birth.... To the laborer in the sweat of his labor, the raw stuff on his anvil is an adversary to be conquered. So was wilderness as adversary to the pioneer. But to the laborer in repose, able for the moment to cast a philosophical eye on his world, that same raw stuff is something to be loved and cherished, because it gives definition and meaning to his life. This is a plea for the preservation of some tag-ends of wilderness, as museum pieces, for the edification of those who may one day wish to see, feel, or study the origins of their cultural inheritance.... Physical combat between men and beasts was...an economic fact, now preserved as hunting and fishing sport. Public wilderness areas are, first of all, a means of perpetuating, in sport form, the more virile and primitive skills in pioneering and subsistence.... A science of land health needs, first of all, a base datum on normality, a picture of how healthy land maintains itself as an organism.... Wilderness, then, assumes

unexpected importance as a laboratory for the study of land-
health.... Only those able to see the pageant of evolution can be
expected to value its theater, the wilderness, or its outstanding
achievement, the grizzly. But if education really educates, there
will, in time, be more and more citizens who understand that
relics of the old West add meaning and value to the new....
Ability to see the cultural value of wilderness boils down, in the
last analysis, to a question of intellectual humility.... It is the
scholar who understands why the raw wilderness gives definition
and meaning to the human enterprise."

So wrote Aldo Leopold in his, *A Sand County Almanac*
(1966).

* * * * *

"This Family is Supported by Timber Dollars." (bumper
sticker, anonymous)

* * * * *

It's a well-constructed house, with perfectly plumbed and
squared walls made of 2x6 wood studs, double-paned, wooden-
framed windows, and good insulation. The energy bills should
be low. And that'll help offset the summer water bills. It's a big
yard, with a lot of grass to mow. There're two extra bedrooms
and you can start thinking about a family now. There's also a
huge living room window, looking out onto the distant wooded
hills. In the comfort of your home you'll be able to view the
changing seasons. And with a little luck, a deer might be seen,
maybe an eagle. It's quite the view. Well worth the price.
You've worked hard for it. You finally have your own home.

The Give-Away[22]

It's your first trip out, into the hills, past the old cabin.
Your father and his father before him had told, seemingly

---

[22]For additional information, see Frey 1987, Nelson 1983, and
Speck 1935.

countless times, of their own "adventures" in those hills. Now it'll be your turn to start the stories. Your gear is ready--good warm boots and a heavy coat, several ham sandwiches, and the family rifle with plenty of ammunition. All that's needed is a good night's rest. It'll be an early start. And now you dream.

As the sun rises over the hill, the crisp image of the morning's frost hangs in the air and from the brush. You continue over each hill, your eyes navigating your feet through and over the deep ruts of the road. The old cabin is not far off now.

The sound comes from your left. You stand there, still, your eyes now searching the horizon. It's a "pronghorned, bull elk." It stands there, still, its eyes watching yours, not more than twenty yards away. In that place, the elk and you share in the sound of heart beats, and in the sight of frozen breath suspended in the air.

You pull out your rifle. Without so much as a flinch, the elk allows you to draw a bead on him. Eye to eye and with a steady aim, the trigger is pulled.

* * * * *

There are four brothers..[23]
"Let's see who will live the longest,
          who will be the most successful,
                    gain honors," they say.
"We'll worship in four different ways," they say....
One brother goes out.
He prays to the Sun,
          each morning..
Every morning at sunrise,
          he's up,
                    makes offerings to the Sun..
This is what the first brother does.....
The second brother goes out.

---

[23]This story is still told today by the Crow people. For a similar account of this narrative, see Lowie 1918:244-54.

He fasts and thirsts..
He stays out for one,
      for two,
          for three,
             for four days at a time.
Then he returns to the camp.
He goes out again,
      to fast and thirst,
          to give of himself.
This is what the second brother does....
The third brother goes out.
He builds sweat lodges,
      calls men of importance to come into the lodge.
They sweat together,
      they pray together.
He does this,
      that is what the third brother does....
The last brother goes out.
This man gives feasts to his clan uncles and aunts,
      he gives gifts to them..
Whenever he sees his clan uncles and aunts,
      he does this,
          men and women of his father's mother's clan..
He may kill a buffalo or a deer,
      he feeds them.
That is what the fourth brother does.....
The first brother,
      the one who prays with the Sun,
          he becomes prominent.
But this brother soon dies...
The second brother,
      the man who fasted in those hills,
          he too becomes famous.
He too soon dies....
The man who gave sweat baths,
      this brother becomes a chief.

He lives to a pretty good age,
>   then dies....
The fourth brother,
>   the one who feasted and gave gifts to his clan uncles and
>   aunts,

>   this man is a great chief,.
>   with many honors...
He lives to such a great age,
>   when he moves his skin tears...
His deeds were the greatest.....
Since then,
>   the people have honored their clan uncles and aunts....

* * * * *

The initiation and maintenance of all relationships, and, in fact, the social and spiritual status of an individual are based upon reciprocity and measured in terms of what is given. Simply put, the more an individual gives away to others, the greater the acknowledged status of that individual. But the giving is "of the heart," of *diakaashe*, "sincerity," and not out of self-interest or anticipated gain. You give in deference and in appreciation.

At each significant juncture in your life, be it your naming ceremony, a birthday, a school graduation, a successful return from military service, an election to the tribal council, you perform an *ammaakee*, a give-away. Valuable gifts such as Pendleton blankets and horses, expressions of one's *diakaashe*, are given to all those relatives who have helped you reach this important stature. And those kinsmen most important to you are your clan uncles and aunts, the men and women of your father's mother's clan. One does not accomplish an honor solely because of his or her own abilities, but only as a result of the varied assistance of these kinsmen. Their assistance includes the constant offering of prayer for you, the singing of praise songs on your behalf at public events, the offering of sound advice and guidance, and, perhaps, some monetary assistance, and, most vital, the giving of an "Indian name" to you, a name that will protect you all your life. Gifts are given and exchanged.

The more that is exchanged and given away among all one's relatives, the greater the integration with those kinsmen, and the greater acknowledged status one acquires. To simply accumulate material possessions, in and of itself, is not a mark of social and spiritual gain and status.

* * * * *

"A penny given is a penny earned."

* * * * *

For the Crow people, a pivotal metaphor in their world view is expressed in their term for clan, *ashammaleaxia*. Literally meaning, "as driftwood lodges," the term signifies a social unit made up of several matrilineally-related extended families. As you watch the swift waters from a river's bank, a lesson is offered. Individual pieces of driftwood can be seen making their way down the river. Most do not make it without being submerged under an eddy or bashed up against a rock. Those pieces of driftwood that do survive the swift currents of the river are those that lodge themselves together on the river's bank.

As a solitary Crow individual, to try to make it in the swift currents of life, currents full of potential adversaries at every juncture, is an impossibility. Only by depending upon each other, by a lodging together of social and of spiritual kinsmen, will each individual survive and prosper. The clan is one such lodging together. Throughout life, the individual seeks to maintain and to initiate anew an extensive web of family ties, ties both with human kinsmen, clan uncles and aunts, for example, and with spiritual kinsmen, a guardian spirit. Kinship is to be found and nurtured among all the "peoples," be they human, animal, bird, plant or spirit. All are part of the lodging of the driftwood.

* * * * *

"The Earth and myself are of one mind."
So spoke Chief Joseph (1840-1904) of the Nez Perce.

* * * * *

"Divinity is the enfolding and unfolding of everything that is. Divinity is in all things in such a way that all things are in divinity."

So wrote the German Catholic Cardinal and mathematician, Nicholas of Cusa (1401-1464).

* * * * *

Christ is the image of the invisible God; born before all created things. In him everything in heaven and on earth was created, not only things visible but also the invisible orders of thrones, sovereignties, authorities, and powers; the whole universe has been created through him and for him. And he exists before everything, and all things are held together in him. (Colossians 1:15-18)

* * * * *

"All that is in God is God.... In God, no creature is more noble than the other.... Ignorant people falsely imagine that God created all things.... God is in all things. The more divinity is in things, the more divinity is outside of things."

So wrote Meister Eckhart.

* * * * *

Shii hozho--"in me there is beauty."
Shaa hozho--"from me beauty radiates." (Navajo)

* * * * *

"O Lady!
We receive but what we give.
And in our life alone does Nature live.
Ours is her wedding garment, ours her shroud!"
The words of Samuel Taylor Coleridge from "Ode to Dejection."

* * * * *

And the buffalos came cascading over the butte, onto the rocks below and onto each other. The hunters above had directed the stampede, and now the women below gather the meat and skins, that which is accessible, that which was given. The night before, the medicine man had offered prayers and spoke with the

Buffalo people.

* * * * *

Buffalo-jump hunting involved the coordinated stampeding of a herd over a high bluff, crippling and killing large numbers of bison. It also involved prayers. Buffalo-jump sites are found primarily on the northern Plains (Montana and Wyoming) and in no other areas of North America. Buffalo-jump hunting was practiced by Paleo-Indians (10,000 B.C. to 1600 A.D.) in conjunction with the more prevalent arroyo/corral trap method as well as individual hunting. Some jumps were used as infrequently as once every twenty-five years. Paleo-Indians were a nomadic, pre-horse people who sparsely populated the area. Buffalo-jump hunting was not practiced by the peoples we often associate with the Plains, e.g., Cheyenne, Crow, Lakota, who were found east of the Mississippi river and were sedentary-horticulturally oriented while the jump method was being practiced.

There were over 350 different indigenous tribal/language groups in North America, representing a diversity of ecological adaptations, e.g., urban-sedentary, horticultural-farming, fishing, gatherer-hunter, hunter, nomadic. The North American Indian spans a history of more than 20,000 years with a population of over 1,000,000 at the time of Euro-American contact. The "buffalo-jump hunting" method was practiced in a limited area by relatively few people prior to the flowering of Plains Indian culture.[24]

* * * * *

"The bear has a soul like ours, and his soul talks to mine in my sleep and tells me what to do."

So spoke Bear With White Paw.

* * * * *

Go and ask the cattle,... to give you instruction. (Job 12:7,8)

---

[24]See Frison 1978.

* * * * *

It's a rough road we're travelling this day; some would say, there's no road at all. We're in the high mesa-country, open to the sky and the winds. Not much in the way of trees, mostly sagebrush and rock. The rough edge is still, though a woodchuck darts from its perch as we pass. Even the clouds seem suspended, motionless. Then the left wheel of our 4x4 hits a rock, and there's motion. We travel on for some time.

Suddenly, you slam on the brakes and jump from the pick-up, rifle in hand, lifted from its rack. The rifle is aimed to the sky and the trigger pulled. The sound echoes in the silence. The bullet whisks past the eagle. And you say to your partner, "The Eagle chose not to be shot, not to give itself this day!"

With your right hand lifted from the steering wheel, raised to the sky and the flight of the bird, we drive on.

* * * * *

No, do not ask anxiously, "What are we to eat? What are we to drink? What shall we wear?" All these are things for the heathen to run after, not you, because your heavenly Father knows that you need them all. Set your mind on God's kingdom and his justice before everything else, and all the rest will come to you as well. (Matthew 6:31-33)

* * * * *

There are no wild beasts, no wilderness, other than when we fail to give thanks. And then who is the wild beast?

* * * * *

The sound of the heart beats is stilled with the pierce of that bullet. The elk lay there, among the frost covered brush. The meat will go a long way. And you have your first story to tell around the dinner table this winter.

As you approach, you raise your arm and give thanks to the Elk. You had taken a sweat bath a couple days before, "a hot one," and, in prayer, had asked for a good hunt for your family. Your words were of respect for the Elk. And then, the night before you met eye to eye, the Elk had come to you. In your dream, the Elk spoke to you,

"You are to hunt only that which you need,
           and use all that you hunt.
Never take too much.
           and never boast about the hunt.
Respect the animal peoples,
           and they will respect you,
                      give of their bodies to you.
Show respect."
This is what the Elk had given to you.

* * * * *

The sound of the heart beats is stilled with the pierce of that bullet. The elk lay there, among the frost covered brush. The meat will go a long way. And you have your first story to tell around the dinner table this winter.

As you approach, looking down at the carcass, a tear fills your eye. Not knowing why, you utter, in a whisper of a voice, the words, "Thank you!"

Choice: An Epilogue

A man is up in the hills, collecting various plants and roots. He's an *akbaalia*, "one who doctors," and with these plants and roots, health will come to many. As he walks the slopes and ridges, the *Awakkule*, the Little People, pay him a visit. They lead him into the distant mountains. There, standing before a large cave opening, he's asked to choose between two tunnels. One has an ending in sight; the other is without ending. He's to choose between two paths in life. One path is easy, with much reward, but is short-lived. The other is a difficult path, with unknown rewards, but is long-lived. The choice is with the man. He chooses the tunnel without end. And as it happens, he's led on a long life, with many rewards.

* * * * *

My intention in this workbook was never to offer a conclusion. Any conclusions should reside in your own interpretation and clarification of values, in your own ability to eye juggle the stories of other peoples as well as your own story. Nevertheless, I will propose three observations. In the first, I will offer my own eye juggling and interpretation of the previous story texts. The texts will be eye juggled as a collective story text, taken as a whole. The interpretation I will be offering is simply one of many voices, including your own, for interpreting the varied stories of our common humanity. I will then discuss some of the implications and consequences of our values on how we relate to our world, including discussion on the "culture of consumption." And finally, I will comment on the importance and responsibility of "choice" in our lives. This entire epilogue

161

is my own attempt at interpreting the *what* and the *why* of the Dream Animal.[1]

The Great Paradox

My first observation. In creating and living in the world of cultural story, the Dream Animal has journeyed far out of the forest, out of nature. The Dream Animal is separated and estranged from the natural world in two fundamental ways. First, by creating the artificial world of culture, the Dream Animal has erected a shield that more or less mediates and cushions the direct forces of nature from him. It is a shield made up of technological and social fibers. Second, the symbolic process itself necessarily presupposes a separation between the referent and a unit of reference, i.e., between something and something else. In such a process there are an observer and an observed, a self and an other, a subject and an object. It is a shield predicated on the very ability of the Dream Animal to symbolize. The Dream Animal is thus forever set apart from the natural world.

For the Dream Animal, the cultural story of the "setting apart from the natural world" gave birth to six primary and interrelated values. While less apparent in the early history of humanity, with the passage of time, these values would come to fruition and pervade all aspects of the cultural story of the Dream Animal, from the social, ideological, psychological and ecological domains to the ethos and persona. The degree to which these six values influence and are expressed in any given individual, group or society will, of course, vary greatly. Each of the six values can be identified, embedded in the story texts of this workbook. The values are: objectification, gradation, quantitation,

---

[1]As with all "interpretation," that which is offered here is *heuristic*. It is meant to simulate discussion, to initiate discovery, and to increase our overall understanding and appreciation of our human condition. However, it should not be considered as somehow the "definitive word."

secularization, progression and reduction. While the terminology may be new to the reader, the concepts referred to should not be. In fact, each term is rather elemental, and thus inclusive of other, more readily identifiable values.

Each of these six values represents what has become associated with the desirable, an ideal to be sought, and not necessarily what is. Judgements are predicated on them; actions strive to bring them about in people's lives. But judgements and actions as with values sometimes fall short of their ideals and goals.

Objectification refers to a process of presupposing and establishing an autonomous, separate world. There is a reality "out there," an "otherness." And that reality is made up of "objects" existing independent of human and divine influences, and independent of thought and spirit. The body and the mind are distinct and separate. Man and God can from afar observe the workings of this objective reality, but its operations are dependent on neither man nor God. Birds, mammals, trees, landscape, mountains--all the "stuff of nature" and all conceptualized as "objects"--have an autonomy of their own. As Newton proposed, the universe is governed by its own autonomous "Laws of Motion." The "stuff of nature" is compartmentalized into its assigned place, separate from humanity. The domestication of plants and animals, and building of the "walls of Jericho," separating the "wild" from the "civilized," were early expressions of this sort of objectification. "Wildness" and "wilderness" thus come into being. And even among a single, separate species, its members can become separate from each other. Hence the rise of social class distinctions, as expressed at Jericho, of "individualism," as noted by Tocqueville, and of "self-interest," as established by Smith in his fundamental principles of "laissez-faire capitalism." To term a phenomenon an "object" is to ultimately render that phenomenon distinct and separate from the whole. In so doing, that phenomenon can now be "analyzed." And in so doing, that phenomenon can now be brought under "dominion."

Gradation refers to a process of presupposing and establishing a hierarchical relationship with the "other," which is, in turn, conceptualized as subordinate. Be it nature or even another human group, the "other" is often assigned distinguishing characteristics thought of as inferior by the dominant group. Rights and privileges are only granted to a few. The trees and animals of a forest are afforded no rights of their own. In its most extreme expression, the "other" is approached as if to be subdued and controlled. "Be fruitful and increase, fill the earth and subdue it, rule over the fish in the sea, the birds of heaven and every living thing that moves upon the earth." In turn, the "other" has value and worth to the extent that it benefits mankind. The human is the "caretaker of his garden," a garden whose purpose is to benefit its caretaker. A forest of trees is to be made into various products for human consumption--lumber for houses and furniture, parks for recreation and fishing; a forest is made into a "natural resource." In contrast, "wilderness" is given further meaning as a wasteland of "no use" that can, in fact, threaten the very vitality and integrity of the cultivated land. "Wildness" must be subjugated, if not eliminated.

It is ironic that the contemporary "environmental" and "wise-use" movements, while espousing entirely opposite views on the value of wilderness, are both predicated on the very same pivotal values, those of objectification and gradation.[2] Both view natural "wilderness" as somehow separate from and in many respects the antithesis of human "civilization." It is only in their reversal of gradation that the distinction between the two positions emerges. While admittedly speaking in oversimplified

---

[2]The "wise-use" movement began in the 1980s as a grass-roots movement of primarily western-states ranchers, timber workers, private-property activists, and conservative republicans. Followers advocate opening up of protected public lands for private use and oppose most forms of governmental regulation. It is felt that only the private property owner is best suited to manage natural resources, having "its best interests at heart."

terms, for the environmentalist, in wilderness can be found the pure, the noble and the beautiful, a place of inspiration, renewal and the possibility of salvation for humanity; in civilization can be found the dangerous, the corrupt and the vile elements of the world. In contrast and often shrouded in Christian references, for the wise-use advocate, in civilization can be found industry, well-being, progress and hope, and the possibility of forging out the Kingdom of God; while in wilderness can be found either "no use" or a natural resource to take dominion over. And if not controlled, the wilds can corrupt and destroy. Wilderness becomes a place of danger from which the Devil will tempt.

Quantitation refers to a world that is entirely knowable to humans, a world knowable in terms of mechanical, numerical elements. The "other" is quantified. The elementary components of the world are discrete and discernible. There need not be any mystery. Eventually man will learn the secrets of the universe. We have already learned its language, and as stated by Pythagoras, Galileo and Bronowski, that language is the language of numbers. The "life" of an animal and the animal itself are precisely and analytically defined, understood in terms of specific chemical and biological processes, and of its quantifiable actions and dimensions. To know the world, then, is to rely upon the experiences and rigors of the human intellect. Empiricism and rationalism predominate.

Secularization refers to the process of envisioning a world devoid of spiritual significance. In its most overt expression, there is no divinity; there is no transcendent within the world. The source for inspiration, the archetypes to guide humanity, is not to be found in the transcendent. There are no souls in animals, nor perhaps, in humanity. If there is an acknowledgement of a divinity, it is of divinity that may have created the world and set it in motion, but it has since left it alone to its own devices. The "other" is primarily material substance, governed by the "Laws of Motion."

Progression refers to the view that through time the human condition develops into more perfect states. Implicit are the notions of lineal time and of advancement. Time is conceptualized with a past, a present and a future. History is made possible. Advancement presupposes that "what was" is necessarily inferior to "what is" and "what will be" is superior to "what is." New is better. The development of the individual, as echoed by Maslow, and of the entirety of humanity, as Spencer and Marx wrote, are conceptualized as a progression from immature to mature, from basic "survival needs" to "self-actualization," from primitive to civilized, be it "classless" or "capitalist" society. And what is to be known in the world is what is to be discovered anew, or to be invented. The old theory is surpassed by the improved. And a new physics awaits; Einstein was convinced of it.

Reduction refers to the view that there is "one true reality," and that reality is vested in material forms and objects. The material world is the world acknowledged. Literalism and reductionism pervade the thinking about the "other." As Marx proposed, the "modes of production" of a society, or as Smith maintained, the material "self-interest," or as Spencer held, the "survival of the fittest," becomes the driving force of our humanity. For Locke, to know is to have a verifiable and replicative experience, to "touch" the material objects, to be empirical. And there can be no other way of knowing the world. A "flower" is reduced to its "natural qualities," be it biologically described by the scientist or literally represented by the artist.

Another expression of reductionist thinking is found in the conviction that eventually there will be a singular, unified theory predictive of the structure and process of the universe. This universe is defined as the natural world of physical entities; all will be reduced to the truth of this singular explanation. Galileo and Newton were convinced of it.

Reduction not only refers to the process in which the material object referred to by the theory is the "truth," but the theory itself is also reified as a material object and as truth. The theory, in fact, often becomes more "real" than that which it refers to. This is the case when it is asserted that "the written word is the literal truth," or when it is assumed that "the theory of inertia is the law causing inertia." The apple fell because of the "law of gravity." In these instances, the unit of reference becomes the referent. That which the symbol refers to is given a concreteness and reality of its own. It is as if a gourmet chef, who, with great deliberateness, follows his recipe book and then adds one final ingredient to his cuisine, the ripped up pages of the recipe book!

Reduction is perhaps the ultimate expression of human separation from the world, the total emphasis on and enclosure within the reality fabricated by human symbolic activity, by theory championed as truth. The theory is the reality.

In attempting to be "set apart from the world," the Dream Animal thus seeks independence from the "other," from the world about it. The Dream Animal erects "walls" and views the world as if through a "glass pane." The "stone" separates. The more distance achieved, the greater the control and dominion obtained. With control comes the enhancement of the Dream Animal's material well-being. A "rich man" is measured in terms of competition and survival, and in the "things" he alone has acquired. The more accumulated, the richer the man. It's a self-reliant, solitary road the "rich man" travels. Only a privileged few are vested with and granted "ideas" and moral rights. With the "individual," so goes the welfare of the community. Humanity looks out from an ever-expanding world of its own fabrication over an ever-increasing barrier into the world of the "other." It is the "other" of the overt, the literal, the material forms. The "stone" is inanimate. It is the "other" knowable only through the rigorous applications of precise methodologies governed by the analytical mind of man. And once known, it is the "other" brought under "dominion." The quest is to the summit of the mountain and, once there, to look down upon the conquered rocks far below. What then is to be feared most is to fall from the mountain top and to participate in the "wildness" below. What is to be feared is the loss of separation from the world. The values of objectification, gradation, quantitation, secularization, progression and reduction have helped define and, in turn, constitute the world as if seen through a "glass pane," the Glass Pane world view.

* * * * *

Yet, despite its estrangement from the natural world, the history of the Dream Animal is a history of questing and searching for meaning within the world, as a part of that world. Despite its best efforts, the Dream Animal has never strayed far from the natural world. The various forces of nature, be they earthquake, flood, heat, cold, are a constant reminder of its ever-present influence. Food, clothing and shelter have always been ultimately derived from nature, though perhaps acknowledged less so today. Nature touches everyone directly, found at each juncture in the life of an individual Dream Animal--birth, nurturance, growth and death.

While the act of symbolizing at once separates, it also facilitates a return to and a participation with the world. Through an ability to symbolize, the Dream Animal is given an opportunity to observe, learn about and grow in the ways of the world. Lessons, literal, metaphoric and anagogic in meaning, are offered. And it has been in the solitudes of the natural world that the Dream Animal has always found the great spiritual and aesthetic meanings to life. The quest has been to the mountain and to the *axis mundi*, and to the beginnings of time and of creation. The quest continues, and the Dream Animal yearns to return to the place of origins.

In the Looking Glass world view, like the Glass Pane world view, six elemental and interrelated values are given life and can be identified in the Dream Animal's cultural story of "questing to be a part of the world." These are subjectification, equalization, qualitation, transcendentation, replication and participation. Unlike the Glass Pane values, these six values are readily apparent throughout all of the history of the Dream Animal, from the earliest times to the most recent. Each of the six values can be seen embedded in the various story texts of this workbook.

As with the Glass Pane world view, these six Looking Glass

values pervade all aspects of the cultural story: the social, ideological, psychological and ecological domains, the ethos and persona. As with the Glass Pane, the actual expression of the Looking Glass values varies from individual to individual and society to society. And finally, these values also refer to the desirable, an ideal to be sought, and not necessarily what is. Judgements and actions are influenced by these values. People strive to actualize them in their lives. But, any given individual or group is capable of falling short of their ideals and values.

The particular configuration of values I have isolated represents a binary typology. The six values identified with the "setting apart" can be paired, representing opposite meanings, with the six values identified with the "questing to be a part." Each of the paired values is thus the antithesis of the other: objectification/subjectification, gradation/equalization, quantitation/qualitation, secularization/transcendentation, progression/replication, and reduction/participation.

This antithetical relation does not preclude the possibility that expressions of both Looking Glass and Glass Pane values can be found in the same community or even in a given individual. In fact, strands of both world views are interwoven throughout our contemporary Euro-American society. Both are essential to and help bring forth the world you and I depend upon. As was suggested previously, despite the tendency for consistency, a particular configuration of values can integrate, however seemingly awkward, disparate and often mutually contradictory values. To embrace one world view does not automatically preclude the incorporation of the other. While the Looking Glass and Glass Pane values presuppose contrast, as threads woven throughout an entire societal system or within an individual personality, they do not necessarily presuppose exclusivity.

Subjectification refers to the process of presupposing and establishing the view that all things are connected into a singular, unified whole. Animal, plant, humanity, physical, spirit, while overtly differentiated, are ultimately linked as an indivisible whole. All "peoples," animal, bird, human and spirit are part of an all-inclusive "kinship," the world of the *Alcheringa*, the "driftwood lodging" and the "wagon wheel," the world of "Mind" and "cybernetic pathways." There is little room for compartmentalization or for autonomous segments, separate from the whole. "Individualism" can not be rooted in subjectification. The philosophy of Descartes and the assertions of Cartesian Dualism separating mind and body, each as non-reducible to the "other," is incompatible with subjectification. And there can be no areas set aside, set apart from the world, as "wilderness areas." All phenomena are intrinsically interconnected--"Mind" and body as one.[3]

Equalization refers to the view that acknowledges differentiation manifested throughout the whole, and that the differentiations are understood as all fundamentally equal to each other. A plant can be overtly distinguished by its physical form and attributes, its "cell membrane or skin," from an animal and from a human, but as each is intrinsically interconnected with the whole, each has an ultimate equality with the others. This is perhaps best expressed in the imagery of the "wagon wheel." Kinship, rather than class distinction, predominates--all "spokes" are of equal value. No one kinsman should be subordinate to another--no one "spoke" can dominate if the wheel is to continue turning. There is no hierarchical relationship among the entities. All phenomena, plant, animal, rock and human are inherently equal with the others. As among the Inuit, a simple "stone" can hold the secrets of life and release the power necessary to assure success in the seal hunt. One listens to even the smallest of creatures, the ant. A forest of trees is the home of animal and bird "peoples," of "bothers" and "sisters." There can be no "wildness" in nature.

And within this network of kinship, all "peoples" share in a reciprocity with one another. If one is to receive a vision from

---

[3]Phenomena are defined as inclusive of all entities knowable through the senses, thought, intuition and mystical revelation, and are not limited to sensual experience.

the Eagle or the meat from a Seal or an Elk, a gift of value must be given. One offers *diakaashe*, sincerity, or closely follows a taboo and shows respect. The members of the Bandicoot and of the Kangaroo clans each dances for the spiritual well-being of its ancestral totem as well as for the physical well-being of the members of the other clan. And at its most elementary level, exchanges of information transpire between all the component parts of the "planetary ecology." Balance among all the "peoples," and the "ideas" must be maintained. Is not the offering of "thanks" an acknowledgement of the completed exchange of information flowing through the cybernetic circuits? Has the Elk offered itself up to the hunter, or was it taken? "Sedna is to be feared."

Qualitation refers to an understanding that the world participated in is a world oozing with meaning, with "informational ecology," with qualities of significance. The world offers archetypes to guide and to live by.[4] "Ideas" and "knowledge" are "inherent in all things." Seeing an eagle while one is on a long journey is not just a sighting of a large diurnal bird of prey, but the Eagle can signify that the journey's destination will be reached safely. The cross and the circle, originating out of a primordial past, have infused meaning into Christian and American Indian being. "Even the smallest ant may wish to communicate." The world is understood as being not only alive with meanings, but also emanates with a "life-force." This is the power of life and of healing, that which animates all things: plant, animal, human, and even rock or feather. Meaning and life abound throughout all phenomena. The world is neither meaningless, in a void, nor is it inanimate and dead.

It is a world that offers messages and lessons, patterns and

---

[4]Archetype is defined as a primordial model of exemplary meaning occurring *in illo tempore*. Implied is the extension and replication of that model in the actions of humans. This usage of the term follows Mircea Eliade 1954 and not Carl Jung.

models, life and health--if "one is attentive." Of course, one can always choose not to listen to its voice. It is a world of choice, and not of fatalism. To know the world is thus to be "attentive" to its voice, to listen with the "heart" and to "feel beauty" in the "stones, leaves, grass, brooks, and the birds and animals." To know the world is to be receptive to all the pathways of the cybernetic ecosystem. "All true wisdom is to be found far from the dwellings of men, in the great solitudes."

Transcendentation envisions a world beyond the overt, material forms, a world inclusive and expansive of transcendent levels. The transcendent pervades and is within all phenomena. This is the realm of "Mind," the interconnecting pathways and messages of the cybernetic ecosystem. This is the realm of the divinity, the dwelling place of the souls, the souls of all "peoples"--human, animal, plant, rock. "The bear has a soul like ours." This is the realm of the intuition, the abode of inspiration. This is the realm of the meaningful and the life-force. From here, all ideas and thoughts are born. From here, a vision to live one's life emanates. From here, an inspiration for a poem or a painting is born. From here, the power to cure emerges. It was here that Burnt Face traveled and from here that he was transformed. To dance in the *Alcheringa* is to dance in the transcendent. The world is not to be reduced to its physical and literal expressions alone. A "flower" is "spiritual essence" "precipitated," its "inner forms" represented by the artist on the churinga board or in the poem.

This is not to suggest that the physical realm is not also acknowledged. The Dream Animal, living close to the natural world, has always been rather pragmatic. The thorn piercing the finger's tip is most assuredly felt. And the thorn is to be avoided. But the thorn, the finger and the pain, the lesson of avoidance are after all given their very existence out of the structures and animations emanating from the transcendent. In the Looking Glass world, the beauty and meaning of the flower cannot be reduced to its physical properties. Thus, as the physical is the overt manifestation of the inner transcendent meanings, the spiritual and aesthetic are always of primary concern. The physical is epiphenomenal of the transcendent.

In "questing to be a part of the world," spiritual self-actualization necessarily precedes material actualization. When the soul is nourished first, so then will the body be given an opportunity to fully grow and prosper. This particular view may seem reversed from what we typically take for granted. But we must be cautious in our assumptions. While those assumptions may be appropriate within certain societal contexts, they may not be appropriate in assisting us in understanding all of the human condition. For instance, we must be cognizant of a dominant praxis premise within Euro-American society that assumes that ideas and a spiritual transcendent are epiphenomenal of the material conditions, e.g., the economic "modes of production" are primary and determinant of societal and religious values. In the example of Maslow's "hierarchy of needs," it is asserted that positive personal adjustment comes only after basic physiological needs such as food and shelter are first achieved. Such an assertion may be not only inappropriate but, in fact, may distort attempts at appreciating the Dream Animal and ourselves in our entirety.

Discussion of transcendentation allows us an opportunity to address a fundamental existential dilemma. As previously suggested, phenomena can be simultaneously unique, differentiated and multiple (equalization presupposes differentiation of divisible parts) as well as united within a singular whole as one (subjectification presupposes an indivisible whole). How can something be *many* and *one* at the same time? A case in point is the symbolism of the spokes and hub of the Crow "wagon wheel" imagery. In the Looking Glass world, this apparent contradiction can be clarified and resolved when the transcendent is brought into consideration. Simply put, the multiple of phenomena is associated with the overt and the manifest, while the oneness of phenomenon is associated with the transcendent. While boundaries demarcate and separate the "conspecific individuals" within the bioenergetic ecology, a unity of interconnected information pathways encloses the entirety of the cybernetic ecology; Mind and body are unified.

The parable of the "mountain climb" further illustrates this resolution. On the mountain there are many and differing routes for reaching the summit. One route comes out of the hot desert, another from the grassland prairie, one from a lush jungle, and a fourth comes out of a rugged mountain range. As each climber begins his or her ascent of the mountain, each is attired in the clothes and gear appropriate to his or her home terrain. Each necessarily differs from the other, unsuited to the terrains of the others. As the climbers continue toward the summit, much of the gear each once wore is discarded along the way. After much effort, each of the climbers finally reaches their common goal. And what each is now wearing is indistinguishable from the others. In our metaphor, the home terrains represent the unique and multiple found in the history and geography of a people, the overt and manifest differences that separate. The summit, reached only "after much effort," represents the unity and oneness to be found in the transcendent.

Replication refers to the view that events and periods of time are continually reoccurring within a pattern of cyclical time. Implicit are the notions of cyclical time and of perennial archetype. Time is conceptualized as continually reoccurring cycles rather than as unique events occurring in a lineal progression, with a past, present and future. "What was" and "what will be" is "what is." It is the *Alcheringa*. And the ancestors continue to "live" among the living. In contrast, "history means disrespect for the ancestors." These reoccurring events and periods of time, in turn, are replications of the perennial archetypes originating out of the transcendent. The beauty of the flower now held in hand is a reflection of the perennial archetypical "flower." One dances the Dreamtime. And what is to be known is ultimately what is to be remembered that had been forgotten--anamnesis. To know is to return to the archetype, to the Dreamtime. For there is "nothing new under the Sun."

Participation refers to the process in which humanity partakes of an active role in helping bring forth the world. Are we not what we imagine? Is not imagination the "act of knowing and of feeling the life within all the world, and of participating in that life?" Is not the "vital act" the "act of participation?" And is not the universe "brought into being by the participation of those who participate?" Given the unity of all creation, and the meaning and animation that emanates through and from it, humanity, as a part of that creation, must necessarily emanate with that same meaning and animation. In turn, the participation of humanity in the world, expressed in symbolic actions, assists in the unfolding and creation of that world. The movement of an Eagle feather can knock over, and it can revive. A name can bring health or it can sicken. The Holy People think the world and then speak the world into being; and God said, "Let there be light." "That which comes through the mouth, words, has the power to effect the world," *dasshussua.* Symbols are creative.

But the human acts of creation are not random, but guided by *perennial, transcendent archetypes.* The animation and the meaningfulness of human symbols occur when the human is in alignment as a microcosm of the world macrocosm, each mirroring the other.[5] The transcendent, and the archetypical meaning and animation that emerge from it, must be equally shared by human and world alike. To receive a vision, one must listen to the animals speak and to one's own soul speak. To receive a poem, one must listen to the voices of the flowers and clouds and to one's own voice. During a vision or an inspiration, all voices are in harmony. To heal with the feathers of the eagle, the symbolic actions of the healer must replicate the archetypical meaning of health as defined in the transcendent and shared by patient, healer, Eagle and the world. To continue through life with meaning, humanity must continually replicate in its actions the archetypical meanings that emanate from the transcendent, in

[5]Much is owed to Mircea Eliade 1954 for clarifying the process and significance of replicating and mirroring archetypes.

humanity itself and from the world. To ignore the archetypes is to be blinded and lost. Symbols are creative when the symbols replicate the transcendent archetypes. And the stone of Sedna was held in one hand and the harpoon in the other. "Then the seal comes forth for a breath of air..., and some fresh water!"

In "questing to be a part of the world," the Dream Animal thus seeks participation with the world. From the transcendent emerge the meanings that guide and the animation to give life to those meanings. The "stone," alive, "held in hand," reveals. But one must be "attentive" with the "heart." To know is to "feel beauty" within the world. And to represent that "beauty" is to attempt to convey the mystery of the "inner forms." To continue access to the meaningful and to life, the Dream Animal seeks to replicate, seeks to mirror, in its actions and deeds the transcendent archetypes that emanate from all of creation--human and animal alike. To look out into the world, to look into the "looking glass," is to see the world within. The quest is to the summit of the mountain, and once there, to continue to live under the shadow of that mountain. What then is to be feared most is to live other than under the shadow, to be estranged from the world and not to participate. What is to be feared is the possibility of "wilderness" itself. In turn, a "rich man" is measured in terms of relationship and reciprocity, and in what is given. The more given the richer the man. A "rich man" becomes a rich kinship, an integral and vital participant in the all-inclusive community of "people"--human, natural and divine. The "ideas" and moral rights of all "peoples" are affirmed. With the "community," so goes the welfare of the individual. The values of subjectification, equalization, qualitation, transcendentation, replication and participation have helped define and in turn constitute the world as if seen through a "looking glass," the Looking Glass world view.

* * * * *

The entirety of the human experience has been a history of oscillating tendencies and pulls, what I have come to term, the Great Paradox. To survive in the natural world and to enhance its material well-being, the Dream Animal has sought to erect "stone walls" and thick "glass panes" between itself and that world, to be estranged from the world, from the natural world, and to live in the Glass Pane world. The Dream Animal has sought to live *apart from the world.* Yet, to obtain ultimate meaning and purpose in life, the Dream Animal has sought membership and participation in the world, to view out into the "looking glass" and see within, to live in the Looking Glass world. The Dream Animal has sought to be *a part of the world.* The stories we have just eye juggled certainly reflect the values of both tendencies. It is this tension and the oscillating emphasis from one to the other tendency, the Great Paradox, which characterizes much of the history of humanity's relationship with the world as well as the difficult choices each individual must make in his or her own life. The Dream Animal, indeed, is a Great Paradox.

The Culture of Consumption

My second observation. In the whole of human history there has never been a societal system that has produced such a *high level of material well-being and wealth of material comforts* than that which has originated out of our modern Euro-American (Western Europe and North America) society.[6]   From sophisticated health care systems, to automated industrial manufacturing, to high-yield farming practices, to expansive transportation and communication networks, to an accessible educational system, the accomplishments go on. Humanity has now walked the craters of the moon and extended the life of a child with the implantation of a baboon's heart. In fact, the human biological heart can now be replaced with a mechanical

---

[6]Our Euro-American society is the culmination of the influences of both Looking Glass and Glass Pane world views. We are reminded that we should not arbitrarily assume an exclusive association of one or the other world view with any particular society.

heart.

The world is rapidly becoming a singular community. What is news in Beijing, Buenos Aires, Jakarta, Moscow or Tokyo is news in one's own living room. And what is dreamed in Beijing, Buenos Aires, Jakarta, Moscow or Tokyo is dreamed in one's own home. The aspirations associated with Euro-American society are rapidly becoming the aspirations of much of the entire world community. And those expectations are directed at ever increasing levels of consumer goods and material well-being, e.g., automobiles, clothing apparel, entertainment systems, recreational equipment, housing, nutrition and health care. One of America's most lucrative exports is its multi-billion-dollar-a-year "Hollywood Image,"--the motion picture, television, magazine, amusement park, popular music, and most assuredly, "fast food" and clothing industries. At this very moment it is likely that someone in Beijing, Buenos Aires, Jakarta, Moscow or Tokyo is standing in a line, wearing a pair of Levis, listening to "rock 'n' roll" and about to order a Big Mac and a Coke, and that someone is not an American. An entire life style, "American Popular Culture," is being successfully marketed worldwide. The images are clearly disseminated and received, images ingrained with expectations.

With the emergence of modern Euro-American society has emerged what John Bodley has labeled the "culture of consumption."[7] It is a life style predicated not only on what one consumes, but on an ever increasing level of consuming. One's social and economic status, familial relationships and modes of entertainment, the very core of one's self-identity are defined in terms of an almost insatiable hunger for consumable goods. Two favorite American pastimes, viewing television and visiting shopping malls, are oriented around their sales pitches for and lure of a seemingly endless array of brightly packaged consumer

---

[7]See Bodley 1985. Bodley is among many who have used the term "culture of consumption." For an insightful discussion of the range and implications of the consumer life style, see Alan Durning 1992.

goods and throwaway products. The "culture of consumption" can best be epitomized in the soft drink and fast food slogans, "Gotta have it" and "What you want is what you get."

With these levels of material well-being and expectation also come a price tag. Never in the whole of human history has a societal system necessitated such high levels of resource and energy consumption than that required by our modern Euro-American society. To facilitate this cultural infrastructure and level of expectation, expanded and new sources of energy and resources are constantly being sought. In 1991, the energy use in the United States translated into the equivalent of each American consuming 25 barrels of oil, 3.5 tons of coal, and 75,000 cubic feet of natural gas.

But within the global community, shared by so many world views, the benefits of Euro-American society are not uniformly bestowed on all those who aspire its dream. While estimations vary, in the United States alone, Americans consume some 40% of the world's annual production of goods and 35% of the world's energy. Americans represent only 5% of the world's population. In global terms, the top 20% of the world's population controls 80% of the wealth while the bottom 20% controls less than 1.5% of the world's wealth. It is estimated that over a billion people in the southern hemisphere of this world survive on the equivalent of one dollar a day. Many dream the dream, yet for most the dream is far from realized. All indications suggest that this socio-economic schism is widening and becoming more pervasive throughout the world, expressed in virtually all communities. The rich are getting richer and the poor are getting poorer.

With the increased levels of energy consumption characteristic of our Euro-American society, the questions remain whether the earth can continue to supply the energy resources necessary to maintain the expectations of its people, and whether the by-products of this level of energy consumption (i.e., pollution) can safely be absorbed within the world ecological system. Are new resources to be found? Are new technologies to be discovered? Is a change in expectations or even world-view values necessary?

At stake are the reserves of fossil fuels and raw materials such as iron ore and copper. At stake is the very fertility of the earth. Within the United States, for every ton of wheat harvested from the great plains, two tons of topsoil are lost because of erosion caused by modern farming practices. Each year some three billion tons of topsoil are lost to water and wind erosion tied to agricultural practices. In turn, agriculture and silviculture account for 46% of all river pollution in the United States. It takes approximately 500 years to produce an inch of topsoil.

At stake is the quality of the air and water. At stake are the global fluctuations in temperature and solar radiation. Each year, America emits over five billion tons of carbon dioxide into the atmosphere, a major "green house" gas, and hundreds of millions of tons of sulfur dioxide, causing acid rain.

At stake is the continued existence of the vast forests of the Amazon, Southeast Asia, and the American Northwest. At stake is the diversity of animal and plant species, and the indigenous peoples who inhabit those forests. Each year between 20,000 and 40,000 species of animals and plants is eliminated from this planet by the actions of humans; and the rate of species extinction is increasing. It is estimated that one in eight known plant and animal species will be extinct within the next ten years. Of the five million Indians who once lived in the Amazon region, only 220,000 survive today. Until very recent and reluctant intervention by the Brazilian and Venezuelan governments, an average of one Yanomami Indian was killed each day by gold mining and lumber interests. Yet, of the remaining 300 million indigenous people scattered throughout the world today, representing some 5% of the world's population, tens of thousands continue to die each year because of murder and warfare or disease and starvation, all brought about as a direct result of the resource demands of Euro-American society. With the death of indigenous peoples comes the loss of cultural diversity. As the biologist reminds us and as echoed in the voice of the anthropologist, a viable ecological system is a reflection of species and cultural diversification. Ultimately all successful adaptations to the dynamic of our bioenergetic-cybernetic niche are predicated on the vitality of and accessibility to system-wide diversity. An unstable and potentially dying ecological system is a reflection of an absence of species and cultural diversification, and the emergence of what is called a "mono-culture."

At stake is not only the quality of our life, but the very existence of the Dream Animal itself. At stake is not only the preservation of pristine wilderness areas, but the very existence of all life in this planetary ecosystem. Never in the history of this planet has a single species so influenced the very survival of all the species!

The Mobius Strip

Long ago a servant was sent to the market to buy some salt and flour for his Lord. "Here, bring the flour and salt to me on this plate, but don't mix the two; keep them separate," the Lord says, handing the plate to his servant. So the servant heads to the market, mindful of these instructions.

At the market, the servant has a shopkeeper fill the plate with flour. But as the shopkeeper is about to measure the salt, the servant stops him. He remembers what his master had told him. So the servant turns the plate over and has the shopkeeper pour the salt on the bottom side of the plate. Careful not to spill any of his cargo, the servant proudly returns to his Lord.

"Here's what you asked me to bring you," the servant says. And he presents the Lord with the plate of salt. "But where's the flour?" commands the Lord. "It's here," says the fool, turning over the plate. But nothing is there, and as soon as the plate is turned, the salt is gone as well!

So it is, in doing one thing that you think to be right, you may undo another which is equally right.

* * * * *

My third observation.   Exclusivity breeds destruction.
Patterns of exclusivity pervade our thinking.   They are often
manifested in dichotomized, either/or thinking such as is found
in situations characterized in terms of us/them, friend/foe,
good/evil, win/loose, true/false, black/white. In these situations
of polar opposites, any given position or category is arbitrarily
perceived as not the other and is excluded from it. However,
when dichotomized thinking is taken to extremes it can
stereotype, distort, limit choices and options, and is divisive. In
the instance of the Glass Pane and the Looking Glass world
views, when one world view has dominated the values of a
particular society or individual, exclusive of the other, the earth
and humanity have suffered.

To embrace Looking Glass values, exclusive of Glass Pane
values, is to ignore the welfare of humanity. The creation and
accessibility of food, shelter, health care, communication,
transportation, recreation: all are contingent upon Glass Pane
values.   The understandings of our biological, historical and
social being as well as the attempts to thwart those stereotypes,
prejudices and hatreds driven by our blind ignorance and false
assertions: all are contingent upon Glass Pane values. "History,"
after all, has chronicled the considerable and senseless destruction
of human and animal "peoples" in the name of "religion," or
"Manifest Destiny," or some other narrowly-defined conviction.
And we are reminded that much of the impetus for the
emergence of our contemporary "social sciences" was the
challenge to the prevailing and pervasive oppression of other
peoples--African American, American Indian, Jew.[8] Certainly
the very assumptions upon which you have endeavored in this
workbook, to "interpret," to "eye juggle," are in part grounded in
Glass Pane values. Our sciences and technologies, our analytical

---

[8]As in the example of the American anthropologist Franz Boas
(1858-1942) and the American sociologist and educator W. E. B. Du
Bois (1868-1963).

pursuits and intellectual curiosities are all thus made possible. Glass Pane values bring forth a world of discovery, as new frontiers are to be explored, and a world of hope, as obstacles to human betterment are overcome. Human populations need the nourishments that Glass Pane values provide.

On the other hand, to embrace Glass Pane values, exclusive of Looking Glass values, is also to ignore the welfare of humanity as well as the welfare of all the earth. When animal, plant and human are defined as material objects alone, and are denied a spirit and soul, are denied "Mind," they are rendered susceptible to neglect, abuse, degradation and destruction. It is so much easier to cut down a stand of trees, endanger a species of animal, and pollute a stream when that tree, animal and stream are seen as nothing more than objects. It is so much easier to hate another person, to be a racist, and to engage in war when that person is seen as nothing more than an object. While the causes of prejudice, whether directed at human or animal "peoples," are certainly varied and numerous, the necessary precondition for them all is objectification. And the greater the objectification, the greater the potential for abuse.

Paradoxically, while Glass Pane values at once bring forth new understandings upon which we as a humanity depend, those understandings are also predicated on the very same values of which we must also be cautious. For those values, when untempered by Looking Glass values, have ultimately fostered our insidious hatreds and wanton destructions of other "peoples." As two expressions of that destruction, we are further reminded that our emerging "social sciences" also contributed to and, however unwittingly, became instruments of European and American colonialism, and of racist doctrine.[9]

And "*the creature that wins against its environment destroys*

---

[9]As in the instances of Herbert Spencer (1820-1903), the German writer Count Joseph Arthur de Gobineau (1816-1882), the English eugenicist Francis Galton (1822-1911), and the American sociologist William Graham Summer (1840-1910).

itself." In our cybernetic ecosystem, the continued viability of any given component, as well as the viability of the complete and total circuit, are dependent of the free flows and exchanges of information through *all* pathways and among *all* components. As the wheel fails to roll when some of its spokes are removed, so too within a closed ecosystem. When segments of the circuitry are ignored or eliminated, entropy and chaos ensue, and death is assured. The Inuit "peoples" maintain a balance in their delicate ecosystem by entering into an *all-inclusive* web of feedback loops and information exchanges with the animal "peoples," regulated in the character of Sedna and an intricate series of hunting taboos. The driftwood survives the turbulence because of the lodging of *all* the driftwood.

And should not the moral rights of *all* "peoples" be acknowledged and assured?

The Looking Glass values necessitate a participation with animals, plants and culturally distinct peoples, with the entirety of the planetary ecology. Brought forth is a world of kinship, as an ethic of respect and cooperation among kinsmen is fostered, and a world of inspiration and imagination, as the ultimate destiny and purpose of the Earth and of Humanity, each inseparable, is revealed and given meaning. Brought forth is the world of the *Alcheringa* and of "Mind." The Earth and Humanity need the nourishments that aesthetic inspiration, spiritual revelation, and ecological humility and balance provide; the Earth and Humanity need what Looking Glass values provide.

* * * * *

Is exclusivity an inevitable feature of our humanity? Or can one category, seemingly an opposite, embrace and be included along side the other? Are we as the fool? Or can we carry the salt and the flour together on the same plate, without spilling one or the other or both?

I am reminded of the Mobius strip.[10]   When can two

---

[10]After August F. Mobius, a German mathematician who died in 1868.

parallel lines, each never crossing over the other and each with a discrete beginning and end, become a singular line, each inclusive of the other, with neither beginning nor end? An impossibility you say? The resolution is, in part, perceptual, in the way we think.

Take a long narrow strip of paper. The outside edges of the strip represent two parallel lines, each separate from the other, each with a beginning and an end--exclusivity. Now twist the strip 180-degrees and link one end with the other. Out of an exclusive, lineal structure of two parallel lines you have created an inclusive circular flow of a singular line, without beginning nor end--inclusivity.

As an expression of our perception of the world, as an ingrained value within our cultural story, I would argue that exclusivity is neither inevitable nor intransigent. Are there not many paths to the summit of the mountain? Is not the Dreamer a part of the Animal, and the Animal the Dreamer? Can we not attempt with one eye to see into the Looking Glass while with the other look through the Glass Pane? As the old man with long, black braids juggled his eyes to the top of that tall cedar, can we not attempt to balance our eye juggling?

* * * * *

As we have discovered, awareness of our stories is a task not easily accomplished. Values are never readily revealed. Yet an

informed life is a life with meaning. An uninformed life is no
life. To "live lives of quiet desperation," as Thoreau suggested,
is to be bound in our imagination and being to a life enslaved by
forces unknown to us, to be at the mercy of our ignorance, to be
owned by our stories. With knowledge comes an opportunity to
celebrate our stories, to rejoice in the meaning and beauty they
have for us. With knowledge also comes an opportunity to re-
evaluate and re-combine the values of our own stories, and to
incorporate the values of another's story, if we so choose. With
knowledge comes ownership of our stories and choice; and, with
choice comes the possibility of an improved quality of life.

    As with the choices offered the *akbaalia* when he was visited
by the Little People, we all have a choice in the particular
combination of stories we wish to tell of and to ourselves, a
choice in the path in life we wish to take. Because of the
tremendous consequences to ourselves, to others, and to the
world about us, should we not then take responsibility to explore
the particular stories we tell and to appreciate the values that
emanate from them, to grow in an awareness of who we are and
what humanity is? Which Looking Glass and which Glass Pane
stories are our stories? Which combination of Glass Pane and
Looking Glass stories do we wish to tell? And what do our
stories tell--what are their implications--implications for us, for
others, for the earth? Should we not take ownership of our
stories? Not to take ownership of our stories is to allow our
stories to own us.

    Eye juggling, in its most essential form, is after all the
human art of making choices and pursuing options, of sending
our eyes to the sky and looking in the four or in the many
directions, or in altogether new ways, or in ways forgotten and
now remembered.

                          * * * * *

    "The essence of moral decisions is the exercise of choice and
the willingness to accept responsibility for that choice."

    So wrote Carol Gilligan in her book entitled, *In A Different
Voice* (1982).

Discussion Questions
and Exercises

Questions

The following questions are among those suggested to initiate discussion on each of the story texts of this workbook.

Dream Animal:	1.d, 1.e, 1.g, 1.j, 2.e
Feathers:	5.i, 5.s, 6.e, 6.h
The Tower:	3.a, 3.c, 3.d, 3.e, 4.a
Soul Food:	4.x, 5.a, 5.b, 5.d, 5.t
The Plant:	4.h, 4.o, 4.u, 4.w, 5.n
The Flower:	4.e, 4.j, 4.l, 4.m, 6.g
The Lesson:	5.k, 7.g, 7.h, 7.i,
The Quest:	7.b, 7.c, 7.d, 7.l
Three Hots/Cot:	4.p, 4.q, 4.r, 4.s, 4.t
Give-Away:	5.f, 5.j, 5.l, 5.r, 5.v

1.   The following questions focus on the Dream Animal.

      a.   In your own words, describe the Dream Animal, i.e., what is the Dream Animal?

      b.   What is the significance of the statement, "Symbols replaced genes, and fire replaced fur?"

187

1.   c.   Based upon the information presented in this workbook, speculate on why the Dream Animal came into existence.

       d.   What are the values and epistemological criteria upon which the account and presentation of the "Dream Animal" story is based?

       e.   In what ways is the Dream Animal story comparable with or different from your own understanding of human origins?

       f.   If your understanding of human origins differs significantly from that of the Dream Animal story, what are the values and referential criteria upon which your story is based?

       g.   What are some of the implications of the Dream Animal story on how contemporary humanity defines its relationship with the world?

       h.   Imagine yourself a *Ramapithecus*. What is a *Ramapithecus* wilderness experience?

       i.   Imagine yourself a *Homo habilis*. What is a *Homo habilis* wilderness experience?

       j.   An appreciation of the gatherer-hunter offers, among other things, two important insights into ourselves. First, we invalidate the commonly-held stereotype that the quality of life among the "primitives" is "savagery" and that contemporary Euro-American "civilization" has "progressed." Nevertheless, what lingers is the question of *why* we should choose to perceive gatherer-hunter peoples in such a way? What does that suggest about ourselves and our own values? Second, an appreciation of the quality of life in gatherer-hunter illustrates the unequivocal linkage with expectations. A "simple" technology is not automatically equated with an "inferior" quality of life. Challenged is the ethnocentric notion that the enhancement of the quality of life is a direct reflection of technological "progress" and expanded resource utilization. Again, the question remains *why* we should choose to perceive technology as so primary? What does that say about ourselves and our own values?

2. Imagine yourself living in the Upper Paleolithic and been among those who painted on the cave walls of Lascuax or Les Trois Freres.

   a. As illustrated on the walls of the Lascuax cave, what is the meaning of the images?

   b. Why are human forms represented as stick-like, while animal forms are more realistically portrayed?

   c. In the Les Trois Freres paintings, why do the figures combine human and animal qualities?

   d. Why are so many of these images painted in the depths of caves, accessible only after a difficult journey?

   e. How do your people define themselves and their relationship with the animals about them?

2.   f.   Given your interpretation of the images in this
                story text, which of your own values most
                helped you arrive at your particular
                interpretation?

        g.   Discuss the salient qualities and distinctions
                between "two-dimensional" and "four-
                dimensional" art forms.

3.   Imagine yourself living in the village of Jericho some
        10,000 years ago.

        a.   Why did your people domesticate plants?

        b.   Why did you build the "wall" and what is its
                significance?

        c.   How has domestication affected the way your
                people define themselves and relate to the world?

        d.   How has domestication of plants affected the
                way your people relate to other peoples, such as
                gatherer-hunters as well as people within your
                village?

        e.   Having built a massive stone wall and tower,
                what is "out there" on the other side of the wall
                to be feared? What are your greatest fears?
                What is the nature of fear among the people of
                Jericho? How does that fear influence your
                actions toward the world?

4.   The following questions focus on how humanity and the world are defined.

   a.   What is the origin of the concepts of "wild" and "wilderness"?

   b.   What is the significance and implications of the statement, "The quest is to the summit of the mountain and, once there, to look down upon the rocks far below?"

   c.   What are the implications and significances of the statement, "The quest is to the summit of the mountain and, once there, to continue to live under the shadow of that mountain?"

   d.   What is the *Alcheringa*? And more specifically, what are significances and implications of a world pervasively inundated by mythic story, where every animal, plant, body of water, landform, star and person is defined and embedded within an intricate mythology?

   e.   For the Australian Aborigine, and for Plato, Thoreau and Bateson, what is a "flower" and what is a "person," and what are their defining attributes? What defining attributes do you personally assign to a "flower" and a "person?"

   f.   What is the significance of and the relationship between Plato's Cave, Thoreau's Pond, the Brew, Bateson's "Mind," and the Dreamtime?

   g.   What are the implications and significances of the statement, "the world is emblematic?"

4.   h.   How are the worlds of Pythagoras and Ptolemy similar to and different from those of the Eskimo and the Australian Aborigine?

        i.   For Plato and Thoreau, what is a "flower" and a "person," and what are their defining properties?

        j.   Compare the worlds of Plato, Thoreau and Bateson with the world of the Eskimo stone carver. How are they similar and different?

        k.   What are the cultural contexts (the character of literature and art forms, and the configuration of religious, social and economic institutions) within which the Sedna and the Stone Carver, and the Karora and the Dreamtime story texts are found? You can consult the bibliography in this workbook as a starting point for your research.

        l.   What are the similarities and differences between the origin accounts as offered by the Eskimo (Sedna story), the Australian Aborigine (Karora story), as found in Genesis, and as expressed in the story of the Dream Animal?

        m.   What is the relationship between how you understand the origin/creation of the world, and how you define and relate to that world?

        n.   Is the world and the human being like a "living being, with a soul?" If so, how is it expressed?

        o.   What is the significance of the statement, "the language of nature is mathematics?"

4.   p.   What are the relationships between and the significance and implications of the statements, "It (the world) has no beginning, nor an end, for time is as a circle, always repeating itself," and "Through time, human society evolves into more advanced states," on how humanity defines the world?

      q.   Are the symbols of "survival of the fittest" and "competition" accurate interpretations of the dominant processes occurring in the biological world as observed by Darwin? Are there other symbols and interpretations of the biological world, e.g., cooperation? Are the symbols "survival of the fittest" and "competition" appropriate and applicable to human social institutions and cultural stories? What are the implications of these symbols on how the world is viewed and related to?

      r.   How is the view of the universe, as defined by Galileo and Newton, similar to the view of humanity as defined by Marx and Maslow? What values do all share in common?

      s.   Are the symbols, "man, by nature, is acquisitive,... driven by the desire to accumulate material wealth," "individualism," "survival of the fittest," "competition," and "progress is endemic to human institutions," reflective of innately human qualities simply revealed for the first time by Smith, Tocqueville and Spencer? Or are these symbols relatively new ways of characterizing humanity and thus helping to create new qualities in the human experience? In either instance, what are some of the implications of these qualities on how humanity relates to the world?

4.   t.   For Franklin, Smith, Tocqueville, Spencer, Marx and Maslow, what are the composite defining properties of "person?" Compare that definition of "person" with that offered by the Eskimo, Indian and Aborigine. How are the definitions similar and different?

      u.   Is the world and the human being like a "great machine?" If so, how is it expressed?

      v.   Is the human being like a "great machine?" If so, how is it expressed?

      w.   For Galileo and Newton, what is a "flower" and what is a "person," and what are their defining attributes? Consider the symbols in "Three Hots and a Cot" as well. What defining attributes do you personally assign to a "flower" and a "person?"

      x.   What is in a "stone?" Contrast the significance and meaning of "stone" as defined and used in the "The Dream Animal," "Tower" and "Soul Food" story texts, i.e. "closely examining the...chipped stone," "stone walls" and "stone image of Sedna." What do you personally see in a "stone?"

5. The following questions focus on the relationship between humanity and the world?

   a. For the Eskimo and Aborigine, what is the meaning of Soul Food, or rephrased, what does it mean that "we live by endangering the souls of others?"

   b. What is the significance and implications of the idea of an animal "freely" offering itself up to the hunter on how that hunter relates to animals generally?

   c. How does a stone image of Sedna affect a hunter's relationship with seals?

   d. In the Eskimo world view, what is the role of Sedna in the hunter-animal relationship, and are there equivalent roles in American culture? How does the Eskimo world view compare with Bateson's cybernetic ecosystem (Flower)?

   e. Compare the relationship of an Eskimo and an American hunter with regard to the animals each hunts.

   f. What is implied in the relationship between the hunters and the Elk and the Eagle (The Give-Away), and between Burnt Face and the Eagle (The Quest) that may refer to how these peoples relate generally to animals and the world about them?

   g. What is the character of the human-animal relationship within the *Alcheringa*?

5.   h.   How is the world of Frances of Assisi similar to
              and different from that of the Eskimo, American
              Indian and Australian Aborigine?

       i.   What are the relationships between and the
              significances of the following symbols, "you're
              only the thing in his dream," "our very existence
              consists in our imagination of ourselves,"
              "Imagination is the act of knowing and feeling
              the life within all of the world, and of
              participating in that life," "waves and particles
              are properties of human interaction with light"
              and "The vital act is the act of participation?"
              (Feathers) What are some of the implications of
              these symbols on how humanity relates to the
              world?

       j.   If the world (animal, plant, earth) and the human
              being are understood as each interconnected with
              the other and each with a spiritual significance,
              as a "living being, with a soul," what are the
              implications for how people assume
              responsibility and relate to the world (animal,
              plant, earth), to other people and to the self?
              Can there be a "land ethic" without also
              acknowledging that the land has rights of its
              own?

       k.   What are the relationships between and the
              significance and implications of the statements,
              "Be fruitful and increase, fill the earth and
              subdue it," and "with technological knowledge,
              man is given power over nature," on how
              humanity relates to the world?

5.   l.   What is the measure of a "rich man?" Consider the significances of the following symbols: "the more given away the greater the status" and "*ashammaleaxia*," (Give-Away), and "people are driven by the desire to accumulate material wealth" and "individualism" (Three Hots and a Cot). What are some of the implications of the "rich man" on how humanity relates to the world?

       m.   What are the significance of the statements, "survival of the fittest," and "early man and gatherer-hunters live a nasty, brutish and short," and what do these statements imply about how the world and other peoples are viewed by those who ascribe to such views?

       n.   If the world (animal, plant and earth) and the human being are understood as each being autonomous from the other and devoid of a spiritual significance, like a "great machine," what are the implications for how people assume responsibility and relate to the world (animal, plant, earth), to other people and to the self?

       o.   What is the relationship between the expectations and values of a people on the one hand and their quality of life and the quality of their world on the other?

       p.   What is the relationship between how the world and how humanity is defined, i.e., what is the relationship between the interior within humanity and the exterior throughout the world for peoples of the Looking Glass and Glass Pane?

5.   q.   Does Pythagoras have an ethic based upon an understanding of numbers? Does a modern scientist have an ethic based upon an understanding of numbers?

      r.   What are humanity's primary motivations, as indicated in "Three Hots and a Cot" and as indicated in "Feathers" and "Give-Away?" What are your own primary motivations. How is our relationship with the world affected by our motivations?

      s.   Are we, as a humanity, responsible for each other and the world or are we, as individuals, responsible for only ourselves? How do we balance the needs of the individual with the needs of the whole? If we have a responsibility to the whole (to all of humanity and the world), what is the nature of that responsibility?

      t.   Now that people live by hunting the seal and caribou, why is there fear among the Eskimo? What is to be feared? What is the nature of that fear? Contrast the nature of fear as understood by the people of Jericho and the Eskimo people. With reference to the fears at Jericho and the Eskimo, in your own personal situation, what are your greatest fears? How do those fears influence your actions toward the world?

      u.   If the hunting attitudes expressed in the story of Sedna (Soul Food) and exemplified in the Elk hunt (Give-Away) are indicative of indigenous North American hunting approaches, why is "buffalo-jump hunting" so often referred to as "characteristic" of Indian hunting practices and thus ecological values? When such a position is held, is it not implied that the Indian is "less than ecological" given the "waste" associated with "buffalo-jump" hunting method? Why do we choose to continue to select this unique example as indicative of all Indian hunting methods when it is clearly inappropriate and not typical? For those individuals who maintain that the values of the "buffalo-jump" hunting method are indicative of Indian hunting practices generally, what is being implied in their own values and in how they conceptualize the Indian?

v. In your own personal situation, what is the importance of individual rights (your right to fulfill your own needs) and of collective responsibility (the right of the whole community to fulfill its needs), and how are they balanced, each with the other?

6. The following questions focus on the significance of artistic and ritual symbols on how humanity relates to the world.

a. How are aesthetic and ritual symbols and expressions different from other types of symbols and expressions?

b. What is the significance of the statement, "Those who have journeyed have journeyed far, as you now will witness and participate in the *Alcheringa*"?

6.   c.   What is the relationship of the Eskimo stone
             carver and the stone, and what was the process
             through which the image of Sedna was
             manifested?

      d.   How might the experience of the Eskimo stone
             carver compare with a contemporary American
             artist?

      e.   What is the significance of *dasshussua*, and of
             the relationship between what we speak and how
             we conceptualize and relate to the world?

      f.   Compare and contrast how the images were
             brought forth out of the stone when held by the
             archaeologist and when held by the Inuit. What
             did each see in the stone? How did each define
             the properties inherent within the stone?

      g.   What are the implications and distinctions in
             accessing the world through qualitative-based
             artistic and ritual symbols, and through
             quantitative-based mathematical symbols? What
             are the advantages of each form of expression,
             i.e., what can each reveal, define and give
             meaning to, that the other can not?

      h.   What is the significance of creative imagination,
             and of the relationship between imagination and
             how we conceptualize and relate to the world?

7.   The following questions focus on how humanity acquires and understands knowledge, and its influences on the way humanity relates to the world.

    a.   What are the structural stages and components within the Burnt Face story, and how do they relate to the vision quest experience of the one "young in the ways of his people?"

    b.   What is the significance of reciprocity in the Burnt Face story?

    c.   What are the ways in which the one "young in the ways of his people" gains knowledge of the world? How is knowledge defined, as indicated in "A Flower" and "The Quest?" In considering the Australian Aborigine and the American Indian, how do you personally define knowledge, i.e., what is knowable?

    d.   What is meant by the statement, "all true wisdom is to be found far from the dwellings of men"?

    e.   What is the cultural context within which the Burnt Face story text is found?

    f.   In the Karora story, how is knowledge of the *Alcheringa* imparted and what constitutes that knowledge?

    g.   What are the ways in which the "classroom students" and Galileo and Newton gained knowledge of the world, and how are those ways similar to and different from the one "young in the ways of his people" (The Quest)? How is knowledge defined in "The Lesson?"   In considering Galileo and Newton, and Locke and Descartes, how do you personally define knowledge, i.e., what is knowable?

7.   h.   In the eyes of the Church, what was Galileo's great offence--a new theory of the cosmos or a new theory on the nature of theory?

      i.   What is the significance of rationalism and empiricism on how humanity relates to the world?

      j.   What is the historical and cultural context within which the Bacon, Locke and Descartes stories are found?

      k.   What is the historical and cultural context within which the Copernicus, Galileo and Newton stories are found?

      l.   What is the relationship between how we define and acquire knowledge, and how we relate to the world? In our own field of study and profession (art, business, nursing, social work, etc.), what is the criteria for knowledge, and how does your discipline define its relation to the world?

Exercises

1.   Apply the method of interpretation to the Eye Juggler story presented in the Introduction of this workbook.

      a.   What are the key symbols within the story text?

      b.   Upon what epistemological criteria are the values based?

1.   c.   What is the significance and meaning of looking in the four directions and not trying to see too much, and of eyes as easily at rest at the top of a tree as in the sockets of one's head?

      d.   What is the relationship between the old man with long black braids and the tree, and between Coyote and the tree?

      e.   What values are ingrained within the story?

      f.   Given the perspective of the story, how might "wilderness" be defined?

2.   Write out a story text that best expresses your values on how you relate to the world and on how you define wilderness. The story can be based upon a memorable event, specific place or particular person in your personal life or you can create an original story based upon your imagination. Be as specific as possible, but be concise. Try to limit your text to one page in length. After you have written out your story, ask yourself and write out: what are the key symbols (specific words and/or images used/conveyed) within the story, what values do these symbols refer to and what is your definition of "wilderness?"

3.   Read and individually eye juggle all the story texts of the workbook, recording interpretations and reflective thoughts in a journal. Before eye juggling can occur, the student should carefully read the "Preface," "Eye Juggler: An Introduction," and "Song: A Methodology" in the workbook. Know your methodology. An important key: all the story texts should be engaged (read or heard) before any given story text is eye juggled. Complete the following for each of the story texts:

3.   a.   Isolate and discuss a minimum of two key values within each story text. Use the definition of "values" as offered in this workbook. Interpret the isolated values from the perspective of the storyteller within the story text, expressing the values of others. Ground the two isolated values with reference to specific symbols in the story text. One, if not both, of the isolated values should express or have implications for how humanity defines its relationship with the world, e.g., what might be the wilderness values of the storyteller? If "wilderness" has no meaning for the storyteller, what values within the story might characterize humanity's relation with the world?

       b.   Reflect on the personal and/or societal implications of the story text. "To reflect" is not to summarize but to think about and study seriously; to reflect is to consider the assumptions and implications of a position or idea; to reflect is to contemplate.

                    --Students are encouraged to link the themes and values conveyed in the story texts with personal experiences and previous academic study.
                    --Students are also encouraged to link these story themes and values with current events as they are reported in the news media (print, radio, television).

              Elaborate and discuss the implications of these linkages for our world and for you personally. Your reflection should express your own values on the issues brought forth.

       Leave space in your journal following each story text

entry to incorporate additional reflections later in the term. The meaning and significance of any given story text may not to revealed upon your initial eye juggling.

4.   An effective way to interpret the story texts is through open discussion with others in a seminar context. Seminar participants are asked to divide into groups of relatively equal size. Each collaborative group is then assigned a specific story text and is responsible for presenting it to the entire seminar. Among the activities each group could complete are the following:

a.   Conduct research on the assigned text and provide discussion on the historical background and/or cultural context (character of the literature and art forms, configuration of religious, social, political and economic institutions, key historical personages) for the story text. Select only a segment or portion from the story text to research, e.g., archaeological background on Jericho from "The Tower," cultural background on the Inuit from "Soul Food," or biographical or historical background on Herbert Spencer from "Three Hots and a Cot." Select a segment that you may know little about or a segment that is of particularly interest to you. Refer to the workbook bibliography for initial sources. Library research will be necessary.

b.   Eye juggle the story text, i.e., clarify and interpret the key values from the perspective of the storyteller within the story text, expressing the values of others. Ground the entire presentation with reference the specific symbols within the story text.

4.   c.   Offer a definition of wilderness as grounded
                from the perspective of the values embedded
                within the story text. What is the storyteller's
                concept of and relationship with the world and/or
                with wilderness? What is the meaning of the
                word "wilderness" for the storyteller? Does
                wilderness have meaning for the storyteller? If
                it does not, how is the relationship between
                humanity and nature defined?

       d.   For the assigned story text, continue telling its
                story.   Attempt to focus on a wilderness
                experience or, if wilderness has no explicit
                meaning, on some other experience involving
                humanity's relationship with nature. Create your
                own characters, events and/or landscape to
                illustrate the value orientations and literary
                motifs of the story text. Your continued story
                should be presented in a format that best
                represents the values of the story text, e.g.,
                drawing, skit or play, speech, oral or written
                story.

       e.   Formulate your own discussion questions
                relevant to the story text or select appropriate
                discussion questions from this workbook, and in
                turn, lead the members of the entire seminar in
                a discussion of those questions. One way the
                questions can be posed is through role playing.
                Based upon the story text, assign particular roles
                to seminar members and establish a particular
                situational scenario. Then pose the questions to
                the role players, soliciting their responses based
                upon the values of their characters.

4.   f.   Reflect on the personal and societal implications of the values within the story text. In so doing, members of the collaborative group have an opportunity to express their own values on the issues and topics brought forth in the story text.

      g.   Among the members of your collaborative group, compare the wilderness definitions and stories for all ten of the story texts. How are they similar and different? What values are revealed in the comparison?

5.   Imagine yourself an American Indian, Eskimo or Australian Aborigine.

      a.   What is an eagle and what are its defining properties?

      b.   Does the eagle have any rights?

      c.   What are your primary motivations?

      d.   What is an American Indian, Eskimo or Australian Aborigine wilderness experience?

6.   Imagine yourself a resource developer.

      a.   What is an eagle and what are its defining properties?

      b.   Does an eagle have any rights?

      c.   What are your primary motivations?

      d.   What is a developer wilderness experience?

7.   Imagine yourself an environmentalist.

      a.   What is an eagle and what are its defining
            properties?

      b.   Does an eagle have any rights?

      c.   What are your primary motivations?

      d.   What is an environmentalist wilderness
            experience?

8.   Imagine yourself, along with fifty other people,
      marooned on an island. There is little hope for rescue or
      escape. Because of your charisma and wisdom, you are
      chosen leader and must decide the fate of all the island's
      inhabitants. Those who have elected you leader represent
      a broad range of American middle-class values and
      expectations. Among the fifty people is an enlightened
      clergy, a brilliant engineer, an expert ecologist, a
      renowned artist, an experienced police officer, a
      compassionate social worker, a skilled physician, an
      astute resource developer and a worldly philosopher.
      You have only rudimentary tools, such as hammers, saws
      and hand drills. The food, medicine, fuel and clothing
      supplies that were brought with the group are rapidly
      dwindling. On the island is a vast diversity of animal
      and plant species, including a majestic but rare species of
      eagle, a rather large though common species of rodent,
      and a pathogenic species of bacterium, *Pasteurella*.
      While many of the species are unknown to you, all of the
      species are in an intricate ecological balance with each
      other. The *Pasteurella* is kept in check and thus a non-
      infectious state. The island is situated in the midst of a
      vast ocean expanse as well as on a typhoon storm path.

8.   a.   Who among all the inhabitants of the island will be your most trusted advisor(s) and why?

    b.   How will you attempt to satisfy the life-style expectations of the people?

    c.   Do the indigenous inhabitants of the island (plant and animal) have rights? If so, what are they and how will you attempt to safeguard those rights?

    d.   How will you attempt to insure the long-term viability of the entire island community, taking into consideration the potential for a growing human population, the depletion of natural resources, the disposal of waste products and the endangerment of the indigenous inhabitants?

    e.   If, for whatever reasons, you had to make a choice between the extinction of the rare species of eagle and the elimination and re-orientation of all previous forms of leisure and recreational activities as well as of many jobs and professions, what decision would you make and why?

    f.   If, for whatever reasons, you had to make a choice between the extinction of the rare species of eagle and the deterioration of the people's welfare, a rise in the incidents of dysfunctional family behavior and crime, and you being deposed as leader, all of which is followed by an eventual new social order, though a societal order offering a substantially reduced standard of living, what decision would you make and why?

8.   g.   If you had to make a choice between the
                extinction of the rare species of eagle and an
                increased level of human infant mortality, what
                decision would you make and why?

        h.   Having imagined yourself through this exercise,
                attempt to isolate those values that have guided
                your decisions. As the leader, what are your
                values?

9.   Review the demographic and energy consumption
        information provided in "The Dream Animal" and "The
        Tower." Draw separate graphs for each set of data,
        plotting on one graph the levels of kilocalories consumed
        per societal type and on the other graph the growth of
        human population over time. Compare the results of the
        two graphs.   Also consider the trends in species
        diversification, natural resource availability and pollution
        as suggested in "The Culture of Consumption."

        a.   What are the implications of this information on
                how humanity relates to the world.

        b.   Imagine what the world might be like in the year
                2050. What are the predominate values which
                define and give meaning to that world?

        c.   How will wilderness be defined in 2050?

10.   Select a wilderness issue that fully engages your personal
        values, e.g., protection of an endangered species, loss of
        jobs and a way of life because of wilderness designation,
        etc., and write a letter to the editor of the local
        newspaper. You need to clearly state your position and
        try to convince other readers of the worth of that
        position. The editor will not accept an editorial of more

than 500 words. You do not have to submit your letter to the newspaper editor, but you should submit it to the community of your fellow seminar students.

11. Conduct "original" research using interviewing techniques with a "live" informant. The values of the informant should be distinct from those of the interviewer. The focus of the research will be on those portions of the informant's story that reveal his/her values on how humanity is defined, how humanity does and should relate to the world, and how "wilderness" is defined. The intent is to comprehend and appreciate the informant's perspective, to "see" the world as he/she sees it. The research will be presented in a written format and include the informant's descriptive story as a text that, in turn, will be eye juggled. Identify the key symbols (e.g., significant words and phrases) used in the story text and suggest the values embedded within that story. Refer to "Interviewing," (in the Methodology section of this workbook), for suggestions on conducting an interview.

12. The following key terms and concepts may help point the way to, if not highlight, many of the pivotal values embedded in the story texts. Review and discuss them to enhance your interpretation of the stories.

Dream Animal
Origin/Creation Stories
Dasshussua
We Are What We Imagine
The Vital Act is the Act of Participation
Original Affluent Society
Rites of Passage
What is to be Feared?
Domesticated and Wild Animals

Be Fruitful and Increase, Fill the Earth and Subdue It
We Live by Endangering the Souls of Others
What is a Person, and Who are to be Considered People?
The Language of Nature is Mathematics
Alcheringa
Nature is the Symbol of the Spirit...the World
    Emblematic
Mind
Cybernetic Epistemology
What is Knowledge, and How is it Acquired?
Tabula Rasa
Utilitarianism
Empiricism
Rationalism
Cartesian Dualism
All True Wisdom is to be Found Far From the Dwellings
    of Men
Awakkule
Reciprocity
Circle
Feel Beauty
What Motivates Humans?
Individualism
Man by Nature is Acquisitive
Survival of the Fittest
Hierarchy of Needs
Self-actualization
Ashammaleaxia
Wagon Wheel
Give-away
What is a Rich Man?
Wilderness

Appendix

Cultural Story Project Copyright Release

Interviewee_____Date_____
Address_____

    I, the understood interviewee, hereby donate to the Cultural Story Project this recorded interview, as well as any transcripts thereof, subject to any restrictions stated below.

    If I have also donated related documents, photos or artifacts which I release for public use, I have noted them below.

    These materials may be freely used by students and researchers of the Cultural Story Project.

    Subject also to any restrictions stated below, my interview may be used for research, instruction, exhibition, publication, broadcast and similar purposes. In order to encourage full use of my interview, I dedicate all of my rights in this information to the public.

Related Materials Released:

Restrictions:

Interviewee's signature_____Date_____

    The Cultural Story Project gratefully acknowledges receipt of the gift (tape and any other items donated) and agrees to abide by the above conditions.

Interviewer's signature_____Date_____

Bibliography

Methodology

Barfield, Owen. 1957. *Saving the Appearances: A Study in Idolatry*. Harcourt, Brace and Jovanovich, New York and London.

Dundes, Alan. 1966. Texture, Text, and Context. *Southern Folklore Quarterly*. 28(4):251-65.

Coomaraswamy, Ananda. 1934. *The Transformation of Nature in Art*. Harvard University Press, Cambridge.

Evans-Pritchard, E. E. 1940. *The Nuer: A description of the modes of livelihood and political institutions of a Nilotic people*. Oxford University Press, New York and Oxford.

----------------------. 1956. *Nuer Religion*. Oxford University Press, New York and Oxford.

Geertz, Clifford. 1973. *The Interpretation of Cultures*. Basic Books, New York.

Kroeber, A. L. 1952. *The Nature of Culture*. University of Chicago Press, Chicago and London.

--------------. 1963. *Anthropology: Culture Patterns and Processes*. Harcourt, Brace and World, New York.

Kuhn, Thomas. 1970. *The Structure of Scientific Revolutions*. 2nd ed. University of Chicago Press, Chicago and London.

Lee, Dorothy. 1954. Symbolization and Values. in *Symbols and Values: An Initial Study*. Harper, New York.

Levi-Strauss, Claude. 1963. *Structural Anthropology.*
     Doubleday, Garden City.
Lewis, Oscar. 1951. *Life in a Mexican Village: Tepoztlan
     Restudied.* University of Illinois Press, Urbana.
Redfield, Robert. 1930. *Tepoztlan, A Mexican Village: A
     Study of Folk Life.* University of Chicago Press,
     Chicago and London.
Sahlins, Marshall. 1976. *Culture and Practical Reason.*
     University of Chicago Press, Chicago and London.
Spradley, James ed. 1972. *Culture and Cognition: Rules,
     Maps, and Plans.* Chandler, San Francisco.
Turner, Victor. 1967. *The Forest of Symbols.* Cornell
     University Press, Ithaca and London.
White, Leslie. 1940. The Symbol: The Origin and Basis of
     Human Behavior. *Philosophy of Science,* 7.

Stories

Barfield, Owen. 1957. *Saving the Appearances: A Study in
     Idolatry.* Harcourt, Brace and Jovanovich, New York
     and London.
Bateson, Gregory. 1972. *Steps to an Ecology of Mind.*
     Chandler Publishing Company, New York.
Bell, Diane. 1983. *Daughters of the Dreaming.* McPhee
     Gribble, and George Allen and Unwin, Melbourne.
Berndt, R. M. and C. H. 1977. *The World of the First
     Australians.* Ure Smith, Sydney.
Bodley, John. 1985. *Anthropology and Contemporary Human
     Problems.* 2nd ed. Mayfield, Palo Alto and London.
Bohr, Niels. 1934. *Atomic Theory and the Description of
     Nature.* Cambridge University Press, Cambridge.
-----------. 1958. *Atomic Theory and Human Knowledge.*
     John Wiley, New York.
Bronowski, Jacob. 1973. *The Ascent of Man.* Little, Brown,
     Boston and Toronto.

Brown, Joseph Epes. 1953. *The Sacred Pipe: Black Elk's Account of the Seven Rites of the Oglala Sioux.* University of Oklahoma Press, Norman and London.

Campbell, Joseph. 1959. *The Masks of God: Primitive Mythology.* Viking, New York.

Cook, Earl. 1971. The Flow of Energy in an Industrial Society. *Scientific American*, 224(3).

Coomaraswamy, Ananda. 1934. *The Transformation of Nature in Art.* Harvard University Press, Cambridge and London.

Eaton, S. Boyd and Melvin Konner. 1985. Paleolithic Nutrition: A Consideration of Its Nature and Current Implications. *New England Journal of Medicine*, 312(5):286-289.

Eiseley, Loren. 1957. *The Immense Journey.* Random House, New York.

Eliade, Mircea. 1954. *The Myth of the Eternal Return or, Cosmos and History.* Princeton University Press, Princeton.

--------------. 1964. *Shamanism: Archaic Techniques of Ecstasy.* Princeton University Press, Princeton.

Emerson, Ralph Waldo. 1985. *Nature.* Beacon Press, Boston.

Fagan, Brain. 1989. *Peoples of the Earth: An Introduction to World Prehistory.* 6th ed. Scott, Foresman and Company, Glenview, Boston, London.

Frey, Rodney. 1987. *The World of the Crow Indians: As Driftwood Lodges.* University of Oklahoma Press, Norman and London.

------------ with Lawrence Aripa and Tom Yellowtail. 1995. *Stories that Make the World: Oral Literature and Storytelling of the Indian Peoples of the Inland Northwest.* University of Oklahoma Press, Norman and London.

Frison, George. 1978. *Prehistoric Hunters of the High Plains.* Academic Press, New York and London.

Furst, Peter and Jill Furst. 1982. *North American Indian Art.* Rizzoli, New York.

Gill, Sam. 1982. *Native American Religions: An Introduction.* Wadsworth, Belmont, California.

Hall, A. Rupert. 1983. *The Revolution in Science: 1500-1750.* Longhorn, New York.

Heisenberg, Werner. 1958. *Physics and Philosophy: The Revolution in Modern Science.* Harper and Row, New York.

Jesser, Clinton. 1975. *Social Theory Revisited.* Dryden Press, Hinsdale, Illinois.

Kroeber, A.L. 1952. *The Nature of Culture.* University of Chicago Press, Chicago and London.

------------. 1963. *Anthropology: Culture Patterns and Processes.* Harcourt, Brace and World, New York.

Lee, Richard. 1968. What Hunters Do for a Living, or, How to Make Out on Scarce Resources. in *Man the Hunter.* Richard Lee and Irven DeVore, ed. Aldine, Chicago.

Leopold, Aldo. 1966. *A Sand County Almanac.* Oxford University Press, New York and Oxford.

Levi-Strauss, Claude. 1966. *The Savage Mind.* University of Chicago Press, Chicago and London.

Lowie, Robert. 1918. *Myths and Traditions of the Crow Indians.* Anthropological Papers of the American Museum of Natural History. 25:1-308. AMS Reprint, New York.

Matthews, Michael, ed. 1989. *The Scientific Background to Modern Philosophy: Selected Readings.* Hackett, Indianapolis and Cambridge.

Mitchell, Frank. 1978. *Navajo Blessingway Singer: The Autobiography of Frank Mitchell 1881-1967.* Charlotte Frisbee and David McAllester, ed. University of Arizona Press, Tucson.

Momaday, N. Scott. 1969. *The Way to Rainy Mountain.* University of New Mexico Press, Albuquerque.

Nabokov, Peter and Robert Easton. 1989. *Native American Architecture.* Oxford University Press, New York and Oxford.

Nash, Roderick. 1982. *Wilderness and the American Mind.* 3rd ed. Yale University Press, New Haven and London.

Nasr, Seyyed Hossein. 1968. *Man and Nature: The Spiritual Crisis of Modern Man.* Unwin, London.

Nelson, Richard. 1983. *Make Prayers to the Raven: A Koyukon View of the Northern Forest.* University of Chicago Press, Chicago and London.

Plato. 1968. *The Republic.* Translation by Benjamin Jowett. Airmont, New York.

Rasmussen, Knud. 1929. *Intellectual Culture of the Iglulik Eskimos.* Gyldendalske Boghandel, Nordisk Forlag, Copenhagen.

----------------. 1931. *The Netsilik Eskimos: Social Life and Spiritual Culture.* Gyldendalske Boghandel, Nordisk Forlag, Copenhagen.

Sahlins, Marshall. 1972. *Stone Age Economics.* Aldine, New York.

------------------. 1976. *Culture and Practical Reason.* University of Chicago, Chicago and London.

Sandmel, Samuel, ed. 1976. *The New English Bible with the Apocrypha.* Oxford University Press, New York and Oxford.

Smith, Huston. 1976. *The Forgotten Truth: The Primordial Tradition.* Harper and Row, New York.

Speck, Frank. 1935. *Naskapi: The Savage Hunters of Labrador Peninsula.* University of Oklahoma Press, Norman and London.

Spencer, Baldwin and F. J. Gillen. 1899. *The Native Tribes of Central Australia.* Macmillan, London.

--------------------------------. 1904. *The Northern Tribes of Central Australia.* Macmillan, London.

Standing Bear, Luther. 1978. *Land of the Spotted Eagle.*
University of Nebraska Press, Lincoln and London.
(originally published in 1933)

Stanner, W.E.H. 1959-63. On Aboriginal Religion. *Oceania.*
30(2&4), 31(2&4), 32(2), 33(4).

Strehlow, T.G.H. 1947. *Aranda Traditions.* Melbourne
University Press, Melbourne.

Thompson, Stith. 1929. *Tales of the North American Indians.*
Indiana University Press, Bloomington and London.

Thoreau, Henry David. 1960. *The Heart of Thoreau's
Journal.* Ed. by Odell Shepard. Dover, New York.

Tonkinson, Robert. 1978. *The Mardudjara Aborigines: Living
the Dream in Australia's Desert.* Harcourt Brace
Jovanovich, New York and London.

Turnbayne, Colin Murray. 1970. *The Myth of Metaphor.*
Revised edition. University of South Carolina Press,
Columbia.

Turner, Victor. 1967. Betwixt and Between: The Liminal
Period in Rites de Passage. in *The Forest of Symbols:
Aspects of Ndembu Ritual.* Cornell University Press,
Ithaca and London.

van Gennep, Arnold. 1906. *The Rites of Passage.* 1960 ed.
University of Chicago Press, Chicago and London.

Wheeler, John, et. al. 1973. *Gravitation.* Freeman, San
Francisco.

White, Leslie. 1940. The Symbol: The Origin and Basis of
Human Behavior. *Philosophy of Science*, 7.

White, Lynn. 1967. The Historical Roots of Our Ecological
Crisis. *Science*, 155(3767).

Witherspoon, Gary. 1977. *Language and Art in the Navajo
Universe.* University of Michigan Press, Ann Arbor.

Wyman, Leland. 1970. *Blessingway.* University of Arizona
Press, Tucson.

Zukav, Gary. 1979. *The Dancing Wu Li Masters: An
Overview of the New Physics.* Morrow, New York.

Choice

Bodley, John. 1985. *Anthropology and Contemporary Human Problems*. 2nd. ed. Mayfield, Palo Alto and London.

Durning, Alan. 1992. *How Much is Enough: The Consumer Society and the Future of the Earth*. Norton, New York.

Gilligan, Carol. 1982. *In A Different Voice*. Harvard University Press, Cambridge and London.

Author

Rodney Frey received a Ph.D. in cultural anthropology from the University of Colorado in 1979. The focus of his ethnographic research has been on the kinship, religious and aesthetic world views of the American Indian, with particular reference to their oral literature. He has conducted numerous applied projects with the Crow and Coeur d'Alene peoples of Montana and Idaho. Their elders have been among his most insightful and enduring teachers. Frey is the author of *The World of the Crow Indians: As Driftwood Lodges* (1987) and with Lawrence Aripa and Tom Yellowtail, *Stories that Make the World: Oral Literature and Storytelling of the Indian Peoples of the Inland Northwest* (1995). He is currently professor of anthropology and Director of Panhandle Area Programs for Lewis-Clark State College in Coeur d'Alene, Idaho.